SETTING
THE SCENE

SETTING
THE SCENE

Sally Featherstone

Published 2011 by A&C Black Publishers Limited
36 Soho Square, London W1D 3QY
www.acblack.com

ISBN 978-1-4081-231-40

Text © Sally Featherstone 2011
Design © Bob Vickers 2011
Photographs © Fotolia, Shutterstock and Rebecca Skerne

Printed in Great Britain by Martins the Printers, Berwick-upon-Tweed

This book is produced using paper that is made from wood grown in
managed, sustainable forests. It is natural, renewable and recyclable.
The logging and manufacturing processes conform to the environmental
regulations of the country of origin.

To see our full range of titles visit www.acblack.com

Contents

Introduction: Taking the fish out of water

When you take a fish out of water, it becomes stressed and eventually it will die. Babies and young children, taken out of their familiar water – the security of their home and family life – are also at risk of failure to thrive if the new environment is so different from their home that they become anxious, stressed and therefore at risk. Of course, we are not suggesting that babies will die if they are not moved carefully from their home setting to day care, but there is now plenty of evidence that the right sort of environment will support and even improve cognitive and social behaviour, giving children a start to life that will affect them for the whole of their lives. However, the wrong sort of environment can do irreparable harm, leaving effects that last a lifetime.

A home from home?

How do we make our out-of-home settings less of a lottery for individual families, and ensure that the early years environment is as supportive as possible, and as little different from home surroundings as we can make it, given the nature of resources and the legislation surrounding childcare?

The widespread provision of out-of-home care, and its uptake by parents, increasingly under pressure to work during their child's early years, has resulted in attempts to provide replacement environments where babies and young children can thrive. These substitute environments are rightly regulated and have developed following guidance on the buildings, resources, activities, people and spaces that should be provided. However, the guidance itself may be misinterpreted and the resulting environment may prove not to be the most supportive to optimum development for babies and young children. A recent report on children's wellbeing in England *Early Intervention: The Next Steps*, Graham Allen (HM Government, January 2011) includes the following thought:

The risks of moving children from their home environment to one of childcare at ever younger ages.

> *'The problem of poor fidelity of implementation is now well understood.'*

The author of the report was referring to the difference between the well-meant rhetoric of guidance, in this case in strategies for early intervention, and the equally well-meant reality of practice in settings. There are hundreds of pages of guidance from many sources on what works when providing a high quality early years environment. Why is it that practitioners often fail to get this match right for the young children they work with?

This book will explore the tensions arising from removing children from their natural environment where, at best they are secure, free and self-programming, into an environment where their needs must compete with those of others, both adults and other children, and a curriculum which may not take their individual needs into account. We now have a situation where babies and children, who have acknowledged needs for security, attachment and strong links with carers and particularly their mothers, may now end up spending most of their day with a wide-ranging group of relative strangers. The vast majority of these strangers are conscientious professionals who are often over-worked, usually under-paid and always torn between 'good enough' practice and the ideal of a home from home for each individual baby or child which meets their unique needs.

The problems of putting theory into practice in establishing a caring environment.

Stepping back in time

Let's go back one generation, to the time when most children were at home until they started school. Imagine a young child (perhaps that child was you) secure in their relationship with their major care-giver, usually their mother, and spending much of their time from birth to five at home. This child spent hours in calm and quiet comfort, with familiar objects and people around, sleeping and waking when their body desired activity, food, changing or company. They took walks in a pram or stroller, facing their mother and communicating with her as they visited the shops, the park, and other places in their immediate neighbourhood.

This baby grew into a toddler who pottered around their house and garden, often in the same room, or within sight of their mother or main care-giver, moving around and playing, with plenty of time for self-initiated activities with simple toys, familiar household equipment or found objects. They continued their exploration of the neighbourhood on walks, visits to the library, to friends and neighbours or on local shopping trips, where shopkeepers were constant and well-known friends. The garden was an extension of the house, the kitchen door was open in most weathers, and 'found objects' such as stones, mud, sticks, leaves and seeds were familiar playthings.

The day for this child was predictable and usually calm. The child had a constant model of grown-up behaviour in household and social activities, watching their adult models taking a phone call, preparing a meal, cleaning the house, reading a book or magazine, listening to the radio, opening post, talking to the milkman or the window cleaner. Familiar visitors from the outside world punctuated the day or the week with regular visits, and watching the arrival and departure of the postman, bin men and others gave a further insight into the life of the neighbourhood, the weather and the seasons. Grandparents and other relatives often lived nearby, and honorary 'aunties and uncles' and extra 'grannies' extended the family.

The change in one generation in the children's lives.

Many readers will recognise this picture of a seemingly far away and rosy personal history, an idyllic childhood where everything was perfect. But of course 'distance lends enchantment to the view' and we tend to remember the sunny days and the pleasant experiences we had as children, forgetting the chapped knees, the ice on the inside of the windows, the loneliness and boredom of long days when parents were busy and friends far away, and the frustration of having to wait for adult attention until the washing was done or the beds made. For some, and for some of the time, things were very different, and it is easy to forget that for these children the rosy picture of a warm and caring family was never a reality. For them life was dominated by poverty, cold, solitude and sharp words, sometimes in a situation where they were in the care of older siblings or unregulated or informal childcare.

Formalised care and education

Our concern for these children has become a national priority, resulting in an ever-expanding provision of sanitised and sometimes over-organised provision for children from as young as six weeks, where every child can benefit from the environments experienced by the most fortunate. Governments, in most developed countries, in their endeavour to improve the chances of the most disadvantaged children, promote formalised early day care and education, although the quality, cost and entitlement vary greatly from country to country. Many are also formulated purely as a preparation or pre-school programme, intended to improve children's chances once they start formal education, a practice which sometimes conflicts with appropriate home-like experiences for children. The emphasis on 'preparation' or 'readiness' for school results in a 'curriculum' rather than the natural free-flow of experiences provided by the best parents in their own homes.

> Universal childcare is an ideal, and needs an ideal environment, but political pressures often emphasise 'readiness for school' and formality follows.

Pressure on parents

The pressure of a nationally-funded, entitlement provision for ever younger children (now including two year olds in many countries) has pushed parents into a position where they feel the things they naturally do with their children at home must be shaped and augmented by purchased programmes, formal activities and preparation for nursery. This can involve them and their children in unsuitable activities at too young an age. Conscientious parents feel that their own ability to rear children will somehow be assessed as their child joins out-of-home care or nursery provision, and this is often compounded by the guilt felt by many working parents.

In her book, *The Cultural Contradictions of Motherhood*, Sharon Hayes describes the pressures on mothers as they try to live up to the expectations of society:

> *She argues that the contemporary model of appropriate mothering reflects an ideology of 'intensive motherhood' in which mothers are expected to be both tireless and unselfish in their constant dedication to caring for their children. This situation creates considerable difficulties and ambivalences for women – particularly employed mothers – as they seek to live up to the unrealistic expectations of modern-day motherhood.*
>
> The Cultural Contradictions of Motherhood, Sharon Hays
> (Yale University Press, 1996).

And of course, we now have so many more pressures and opportunities that inevitably impact on the lives of children and families today. Not just many more working parents, but 24-hour communication by TV and the Internet, widespread availability of the computer, continuous distance shopping experiences, and a 'want it now' culture. These opportunities conspire to create a very different childhood within one generation!

Universal childcare can have some other effects on the home environment. In many modern homes, children's toys and activities are restricted to their rooms, where they compete with an ever-present TV picture or computer screen. Mess, noise and complex activities are discouraged by some parents, and paint, dough and glue are left to the nursery to provide. Evenings and weekends are spent in the top 21st Century activities for families of watching TV, a DVD or shopping in vast malls where lights and noise compete for attention. Walks to the park, the woods or other local green spaces are infrequent for many children and unknown for some.

Of course, there is a shrinking group of parents keen to spend time with their children, making, doing, walking, talking, visiting and experiencing a wide range of activities and places. But this sort of life is not the norm for most children, and parents who want their children to have more freedom and be more active sometimes feel conscious of the difference between their own children and their children's friends.

Pressure on parents has changed the balance between the environment and the activities in the home and those in the setting.

Life in the 21st Century

Change in society seems to have speeded up everywhere. We are constantly in a hurry, and innovation seems to be happening at breakneck speed. Life has changed so much in even one generation. Children in the 21st Century, particularly in their early years, often have a very different experience from that of their parents. They are woken early, often before they are ready, rushed off to childcare strapped in a car seat in the back of a car, to a setting where the routines of the day are often dictated by the adults rather than the children and the environment is dominated by 'child friendly' (or is it 'health and safety' friendly?) plastic toys in bright primary colours, cold surfaces, hard furniture, closed doors to the garden, and entrance bells to ensure security. Families are often so pressured that babies and children arrive at their settings sleepy, hungry, with shoes and clothing unsuited to play, and with little time for the proper farewells, which are so important for children at this vital point of transition.

Once inside the setting, the day is scheduled by changing time, nap time, group times, meal and snack times, which only have any flexibility for fortunate individuals in the best settings.

And this environment is managed by adults who are paid solely to orchestrate children's experiences and fulfil the demands of a curriculum written to meet all needs, but in reality matching only those of the minority. These adults, all trained and many very experienced, spend their time observing the children, planning and preparing experiences for them, and maintaining the environment. They have a very different role, as practitioners not parents, managers not models, with a professional commitment to children who are not their own. If the programme is constrained with tasks to do rather than needs to be met, the adults are constantly focused on the children, monitoring their progress against pre-set criteria and always aware of the issues of safety and progress.

The new environment for young children.

Stifling children's independence

It may become apparent in the future that we are producing a generation of children who see adult attention as a right, and have become so demanding that they find it difficult to act independently or look after themselves – children who have been so wrapped in the cotton wool of care that they can't manage any sort of risk, and worse, can't bear to be alone or self-dependent.

How different this is from home, where child and parent often work and play in comfortable parallel, where children's desires and requests sometimes have to wait for the chores to be completed, and parents and children operate alongside each other, often in the same room, but each absorbed in their own activities. Naps, snacks and shared activities are managed with flexibility around the fixed points of the day and the needs of individuals, and where children's successes and achievements can be instantly celebrated in a close environment. Of course, the parent has to balance the needs of the child with the wider

needs of the family, but this balance of closeness with compromise is totally unlike the model of an early years provider.

In our new world, some children experience several changes of environment during the day, moving from home to childminder, to nursery, to minder, then home, reaching this at a time when their parents are at their least responsive or tolerant and most needy of support themselves. Each of the care environments should be of consistent quality, but each is different, with different resources, relationships and expectations, and however hard parents and carers try to agree boundaries and behaviours, it is impossible to replicate the steady, day-long predictability of a caring home setting.

In these situations we are in danger of adding to children's dependency on adults with the insecurity of constant change, a feeling that they belong nowhere. This lack of security adds to children's difficulties as they move into school, putting them at risk of the behaviours teachers find challenging as groups get larger, adults less numerous, and the curriculum more demanding. Many teachers now comment on lack of attention, demanding behaviour, social ineptitude and inability to work alone, as much more common among school-age pupils.

The pressures of multiple environments; children losing their independence.

What is the answer?

So should we try to make the environment in early years settings identical to a good home? Should we only have adult-sized, home-style furniture, equipment and fittings, with a light touch of management of children's agendas? Should we abandon the early years curriculum in favour of something that attempts to replicate every child's upbringing? Should we dragoon children into outdoor experiences and old-fashioned craft exercises?

The answer is a very firm 'NO!' I don't want you to think that I am some sort of Luddite, bent on turning the clock back. I strongly support universal nursery education in a wide variety of high quality settings, and feel that recent developments in clarifying expectations for practitioners and parents about the nature of the experiences for babies and children are helpful. Of course there are huge benefits to a common curriculum, which describes an entitlement and ensures that children from all backgrounds get the same experiences. It should provide the richness that deprived children need, the company that only children need, the order that replaces the chaotic life in some families and a chance to 'stand on the shoulders of giants' as knowledgeable practitioners offer some of the experiences, people and resources difficult to provide at home.

Ensuring equality of provision for all children.

How this ideal experience is described and offered to children is the focus of this book. Not only the *what*, but the *where*, the *why* and the *how* of maintaining childhood environments strong in the social and emotional support essential for children to thrive. These environments need to support, inspire and excite babies and young children, laying down the foundations for future learning and life in a society that, without doubt, will continue to change faster than we can keep up with, and where they will certainly need skills we do not yet recognise.

Providing the right foundations

So how do we keep 'the fish' in the right sort of water to ensure the best foundations for the future, within an environment of care and stimulation, where every child can be sure that their unique nature and unique needs can be met?

In further chapters, this book will explore:

- The key influences on early childhood provision – what some of the enduring thinkers about the early curriculum believed about the environment, and how these thoughts have affected current provision in high quality settings throughout the world.
- The importance of outdoor learning for all children and some thoughts about the outdoor environment.
- The developmental needs of very young children (babies and toddlers) as they make those daily transitions from home to setting, and the key features of quality environments for children at this stage.
- How environments might change to meet the continuing needs of children between three and six as they explore and become increasingly confident and independent.
- 'Observing and watching' – the role of the adult.
- Places and spaces for being and for active learning.
- Essentials – looking at the environmental threads of quality provision.

The research into Effective Provision of Pre-School Education (EPPE) states that a 'potentially instructive learning environment' makes a great and lasting difference to children's lives, during their early years and for the rest of their lives.

> 'EPPE concludes that in the most effective centres, play environments were used to provide the basis of instructive learning. The most effective pedagogy is both "teaching" and providing freely chosen, yet potentially instructive play activities.'
> Effective Provision of Pre-School Education (EPPE), Sylva et al
> (Institute of Education, 1999).

Where this 'potentially instructive learning environment' builds on a strong home learning environment, the effect is even more powerful:

> *'For example, reading to the child, teaching songs and nursery rhymes, painting and drawing, playing with letters and numbers, visiting the library, teaching the alphabet, taking children on visits and creating regular opportunities for them to play with their friends at home, were all associated with higher cognitive and social/behavioural scores.'*
> 'Research Matters' (Institute of Education, London, 2003).

Providing 'freely chosen yet potentially instructive play activities' that build on home experiences.

As our lives change and babies and children spend even more time in the care of others rather than their parents, how can practitioners provide an environment that includes some of the key elements of good parenting, while still fulfilling their professional responsibilities? We must ensure that the 'educare water' is still right for the small and sensitive fish we put in it.

Misinterpreting messages 1

In this chapter, I will continue to explore the concept of '...*poor fidelity of implementation*' because it is not just a current problem. It has affected the process of replicating theory accurately in practice throughout the last 250 years, from the days of Rousseau in 1762, when Emile was published. Maria Montessori and other major innovators in early education also suffered from this lack of fidelity in the implementation of their methods, a sort of Chinese Whispers game, where the essential messages became at best diluted, and at worst distorted as the word spread about developing practice. This effect has been particularly evident when we look at the environment for early learning, and the way it has supported the philosophy and methodology of each education movement as it has spread from school to school and country to country.

Well-meaning and conscientious followers sometimes take unintentional liberties when interpreting the work of those who go before them, particularly after their death, and even more so when the true message is difficult to interpret, overly theoretical, or demonstrated rather than written in handbooks or guidance on practice. The effect of this on the early years environment is particularly apparent when we examine the objects and experiences offered to young children, both at home and in out-of-home settings, and the way they have changed, both in appearance and use.

> '*Unfortunately kindergarten for us and for most generations born in this (the 20th) century was a distortion, a diluted version of what originated as a radical and highly spiritual system of abstract design activities intended to teach the recognition and appreciation of natural harmony.*'
> *Inventing Kindergarten*, Norman Brosterman (Abrams, 1997).

Consider the crystals, leaves, stones, shells and simple wooden shapes used by Froebel in his own schools, or Maria Montessori's child-sized but home-like wooden furniture, and the way these have now become transformed into brightly-coloured plastic, with complex shapes and patterns.

The gap between the rhetoric or theory and the reality of practice can sometimes result in the distortion of essential elements of provision.

Let's take a look at the line of educational thinkers of the late 18th, 19th and 20th centuries, who thought, talked about and demonstrated the importance of the early years' environment. I will concentrate on a philosophical line from Rousseau, through Pestalozzi, Froebel and Montessori, each of whom left a lasting mark on the education of young children and particularly the environment for play and work in the earliest years.

Jean Jacques Rousseau

In Geneva, in 1762, Jean Jacques Rousseau (1712–1778) wrote *Emile* or *On Education*, a book describing his philosophy of child rearing, and detailing the view that education is best when it releases the 'natural child'. No longer were children to be considered 'noble savages' but natural beings who needed freedom and love. At a time when early education was virtually non-existent and women were not considered to be very important, the book caused some consternation by encouraging breast feeding, discouraging the tight swaddling of babies favoured in those times, and suggesting that young children should be introduced to active learning through nature and real objects.

> '*Instead of keeping him mewed up in a stuffy room, take him out into a meadow every day; let him run about, let him struggle and fall again and again, the oftener the better; … the delights of liberty will make up for many bruises.*'
> *Emile*, Jean Jacques Rousseau (1762) (Everyman Library, 2000).

These outspoken words initially resulted in the book being burned, although very soon after, it became hugely popular and widely read, having a significant influence on parents and teachers in Rousseau's own lifetime, and on the many educational innovators who came after him. Many of Rousseau's contemporary followers were women, who saw an opportunity in early education to raise the status of women as well as improving the lives of children. This was the beginning of the movement away from a male dominated teaching profession with the raising of the status of women as professional educators, particularly in the early years.

Rousseau: The need for freedom and love. Education should take place mainly out of doors, through experience of the natural world.

Johann Heinrich Pestalozzi

Johann Heinrich Pestalozzi (1746–1847) took Rousseau's ideas and developed them into practice in the schools he established, where children learned from real objects and natural experiences, exploring these in depth before attempting to describe or use them. He was also among the first to emphasise that the teacher should set up the environment for learning according to clear principles, and then observe the children as they explored the experiences and objects offered. He advocated:

> Pestalozzi: The power of nature and concrete objects. First-hand experiences should predominate.

- begin with the concrete object before introducing abstract concepts
- begin with the immediate environment before dealing with what is distant and remote
- begin with easy exercises or activities before introducing complex ones
- proceed gradually, cumulatively, and slowly.

Pestalozzi fought against traditional didactic methods, and was one of the first exponents of the 'experiential' or 'first hand' methods still supported in early education today:

> *'I wish to wrest education from the outworn order of doddering old teaching hacks as well as from the new-fangled order of cheap, artificial teaching tricks, and entrust it to the eternal powers of nature herself...'*
> Pestalozzi quoted in *Pestalozzi: The Man and His Work*, Silber, K.
> (Routledge and Kegan Paul, 1965).

Pestalozzi still has followers today and Pestalozzi villages still promote his thinking. However, compared with some of his followers and admirers, he was less successful in the wider promotion of his central theories on child education.

Friedrich Froebel

Friedrich Froebel (1782–1852) was born in Germany, and did not become a teacher/philosopher until he was 40 years old, when he was inspired by a visit to Pestalozzi's own school. This visit had a profound effect, and the rest of Froebel's life was dedicated to founding his own schools, writing pamphlets and magazine articles, and, with the help of his protégée and faithful patron Bertha von Marenholtz-Bülow, promoting his methods. Versions of his kindergartens were central to provision in many countries for the second half of the 19th Century and well into the 20th.

Froebel believed strongly that children are innately ready to learn – not *'small stupid people engaged in useless activity'* – they learn best through action and observation of the real world:

> *'Fathers should lead their children out into nature and teach them on the hilltops and in the valleys.'*
> Froebel quoted in *Inventing Kindergarten*, Norman Brosterman
> (Abrams, 1997).

As Froebel worked in the schools he founded, he realised that his methods needed a name, a sort of brand to identify their special nature, and in 1839, he chose the name 'kindergarten' – a garden for, or garden of, children where young minds could be engaged through self-chosen activity, self-expression and play. He described this as 'the work of children'. The name, and many of the principles Froebel held, are still evident in early years education, particularly in the USA where kindergarten now describes the year before statutory school begins.

Teachers in Froebel's gardens for children were providers and observers, setting up the environment, supporting play and replicating the role of a loving mother in children's lives. Resources such as shells, acorns and crystals were frequently used, supplemented by more structured resources called 'gifts', which Froebel and his followers used to help children understand the world about them. This range of twenty gifts (further information from www.froebelgifts.com), were specially made objects for learning, and were a central element of the curriculum. Each gift was explored in turn by the children, with the support of their teachers, to address the three realms identified in Froebel's curriculum:

- Life and nature (exploring the world of nature)
- Knowledge (exploring scientific and mathematical concepts)
- Beauty (exploring the arts).

The gifts could be described as the first educational toys for young children. They were used to represent, explore and define the world, through stories, discussions and manipulation, and using the later gifts, creating patterns, pictures and other constructions. All the gifts were 'table top' size, ranging from the first gift (simple woollen balls on strings) through wooden blocks, shapes, mosaic pieces and other activities designed to coordinate hand and eye, finally culminating in the gift of clay, where the child could construct their own representations of life, knowledge and beauty.

There were suggestions for the use of each gift in each of the three realms, but the gifts were originally intended for children to use independently, with minimal intervention from adults. Written instructions, exploring the way the gifts could be used across the three realms, were almost certainly developed later as kindergarten methods were adopted in other countries and parents and teachers wanted more help in their use. Table-top work with the gifts was an essential part of the day, embedded in other activities such as gardening, singing, playing games, exploring movement and performing routine tasks that 'encourage responsibility, curiosity and a sense of community'.

As we examine Froebel's influence on early childhood education, and on the environment which best supports it, we find that although he was a successful and inspirational practitioner and trainer, he had little time or inclination to write his philosophy down in books of guidance, preferring to contribute articles to magazines and pamphlets, and these were often written in complex and obscure prose. These documents, although widely read during Froebel's life, were replaced after his death by simpler, more practical (and therefore possibly less accurate) guidance constructed by followers, in particular Bertha von Marenholtz-Bülow, who made extensive tours of Europe, the Far East, Russia and the USA to promote the methods. Much of Froebel's direct guidance has been lost over time, and that which does remain, including the principles of Froebelian education, is still maintained within Froebel societies and institutes throughout the world. However, his key messages would be supported by everyone working with young children today:

- 'Each child is a **unique and creative being** and needs to be respected, valued and recognized as an individual
- The **role of adults is central** in protecting and guiding each child. It must be appreciated that parents/carers are the first and most enduring guardians and educators of their children

- *The **partnership between parents/carers** and educators should be sustained and strong to encourage each child to fulfill their potential*
- ***Each child must be given the right to grow and develop**, as a responsible member of a wider community, embracing diversity and inclusion, and be encouraged to contribute to the society in which he or she lives*
- ***Each child's intellectual, emotional, social and physical wellbeing must be fostered**, developed and encouraged, to this end:*
  - Each child's concept of self, self esteem and confidence should be fostered to enable him or her to become an autonomous, creative and original thinker
  - Each child is entitled to a curriculum which provides opportunities for wonder, exploration, excitement and collaborative, purposeful learning
  - The young child should learn through first hand experience, movement, communication and play as far as is practical
  - Each child should have access to a stimulating environment, combining indoor and outdoor learning.'

International Froebel Society; /www.intfroebelsoc.org

In his book linking Froebel's teaching with major modern art and architectural movements, Norman Brosterman says:

> 'Although remnants of the original Froebelian system are still detectable in kindergarten classes today – particularly the emphasis on handicrafts and block play – the gifts, the solemnity in which they were used, and the spirituality they were designed to awaken are long dead.'
> Inventing Kindergarten, Norman Brosterman (Abrams, 1997).

This view echoes our theme of fidelity of implementation, and one wonders whether Froebel would recognise the kindergarten of today. However, as we continue to examine the effect of early educators on the environment for learning, we should remember that Froebel still has an important place in our principles and practice after more than 200 years.

Froebel: outdoor learning in a kindergarten; free choice, natural objects; didactic materials available for children to explore through realms of experience.

Maria Montessori

Following Froebel, we can now explore the influence of Maria Montessori (1870–1952). Montessori gave credit in her writings to the great educators who came before her. These included Pestalozzi and particularly Froebel, whose work, throughout Maria Montessori's life, had a seismic effect on provision for young children across the world.

Everyone who is interested in early education surely knows her name, and even parents who are not particularly knowledgeable about education may select a Montessori school for their child because they somehow feel that the name is an automatic indicator of quality. There are thousands of Montessori schools across the world (8,000 in the US, and 700 in the UK alone) with the word Montessori in their titles, and many more nurseries and early years settings aspire to what they think Maria Montessori promoted. However, there is a word of caution even from Montessorians themselves – all that glitters with the name is not the gold standard!

'Montessori is not a registered name and amazingly, it is possible to set up a school and call it Montessori even if you don't have any Montessori trained teachers and not one piece of Montessori material.' (Montessori Society website)

'Although the Montessori name is recognised by many, it is not a trademark, and it is associated with more than one organisation. Schools and teacher training programs can differ in their interpretation, intensity, practical application, and philosophy in using this method with children'.

Wikipedia

Yet again we can see that the original intentions of a great educator have been diluted and even used erroneously to imply knowledge of and adherence to original methods.

Maria Montessori was born in Rome and became the first woman doctor in Italy. She began her work with children in the area of special needs, working with disabled children, thought at the time to be incapable of learning. She defied this contemporary view, and used real objects, sensory activities and stimulating resources to enable children in her classes to learn to read, write and talk, in many cases resulting in extraordinary results compared with able bodied peers.

Her success using these methods with disabled children encouraged her to try the same methods with 'average' but disadvantaged children, and she opened her 'Casa Di Bambini' (Children's House) in the slums of Rome in 1907. The Children's Houses were set up with very specific resources and equipment, in an environment carefully organised to ensure that the children could develop freely, using the resources planned and offered by the adults. Maria Montessori had a very clear view of what would be effective, and she wrote several books to ensure that the practitioners (and parents who also wanted the information) had clear instructions of what to do and how to do it.

Her principles were to provide an environment that secured:

- liberty for the child, while providing key experiences
- didactic (instructive) materials *and* free choice
- a home-like environment 'A real house with rooms' and 'A garden of which the children are masters', but both equipped with child-sized equipment '... complete equipment for the management of the miniature family.'
- adults whose role was to observe and provide 'Not simply a mother substitute but more an elder sibling, who does not get between the child and the experience'.

'The teacher's first duty is to watch over the environment, and this takes precedence over all the rest. Its influence is indirect, but unless it be well done there will be no effective and permanent results of any kind, physical, intellectual or spiritual.'

Maria Montessori

The house had separate rooms where different activities took place – for instance:

- **The Principal room** or 'working room' where 'intellectual work' took place, with key equipment for storage of the didactic materials and drawers for children's personal belongings. This room had low tables and small chairs light enough for children to move themselves, small mats that children could spread on the floor to work on, and low level blackboards on the walls.
- **The Sitting room** where children could play with table top games, read or tell stories, sing, talk and relax. Key features included photographs, potted plants, games such as patience, musical instruments and a piano.
- **The Dressing room** or wash room, where children could not only dress and undress themselves (including putting on aprons when

needed), but could practise some of the home-making activities, including sweeping, washing dishes and clothes and pouring juice. Shelves, sinks and tables were at child height to help their independence in these tasks.

- The **Manual room** was equipped for clay work, block building and the making of models.
- The **Dining room** where children set tables, served themselves and each other, and cleared away afterwards; the **Gymnasium** for physical exercise; and the **Rest room** (with little beds) completed the rooms within the house.
- Outside was the **Garden** for play, which included gardening tools and activities, spaces to run and places to be quiet and reflect.

It is interesting to consider the extent to which these areas remain as structures for early environments today, even though we might not have the luxury of a whole house, practitioners will still recognise the elements of their own settings. Whether they call these learning centres, activity areas, corners for learning or another name, the different areas have changed little over the years.

The Children's Houses were a great success, children flourished and enjoyed their experiences, and the schools attracted visitors from all over the world, keen to understand the theory in practice. However, the danger of all 'educational visits for teachers' is that a partial or unbalanced picture may be taken away. No method can be transplanted wholesale into any other area or culture. The challenge is to understand the philosophy and see how it could be put into practice locally; even when different visitors will see different things, remember different aspects, and try to replicate different methods when they return home. Without careful thought and reflection on differences as well as similarities between the two environments, the result can be disastrous!

When teachers visited the Children's Houses some only saw the didactic materials and tried to transplant these, others adopted the freedom without the close observation required to support individual children, yet others thought that 'real, yet child-sized' furniture and equipment meant 'pretend' equipment and provided plastic replicas which frustrated learning instead of supporting it.

The Montessori method had a massive influence on early years

Montessori: child-sized, but real furniture and equipment; didactic materials available for children to explore; independence; free play; choice; adults whose role is to plan the environment and watch how the children explore it.

education throughout the world, being the major influence in many countries until the end of her life in the late 1950s, when it was overtaken by the next stage of development of early years practice.

Between the World Wars, Montessori's work became over-shadowed in American public schools by John Dewey's pragmatic approach to education and 'progressive' methods which relied on the work of psychologists and researchers into child development. In many of these movements, practice genuinely attempted to reflect the findings of the scientific world, interpreted by Piaget and Vygotsky. However, it was sometimes difficult to encompass all the different strands of educational thinking, and practice in some settings became confused and the messages became diffuse or muddled as teachers and other practitioners tried to juggle all the advice they were getting.

Jean Piaget

Piaget (1896–1980) recommended that although children should have freedom and free choice, because they passed through such clearly defined stages of development, the activities should be planned to closely match their stage of development. He thought that challenging children with concepts beyond their current stage of development could do actual harm.

> 'Piagetian theory does not advocate that children perform tasks that are beyond their cognitive capabilities. The teacher merely prepares the environment for the child's developmental level of mental or motor operations. Thus, the child is limited by their developmental stage.'
> W. T. LeGard, (Open University, 2004) quoted in:
> www.scribd.com/doc/13401568/Piaget-Versus-Vygotsky

The idea of 'readiness' was inherent in Piaget's work, and this often led to a lack of structure in the curriculum and to a lack of progression in children's learning.

Lev Vygotsky

Vygotsky (1896–1934) researched the relationship between learning and play. However, he disagreed with Piaget in that he recommended that adults should stretch children's thinking and learning, helping them into the 'zone of proximal development', the next level of learning, where they could make real progress. This scaffolding through challenging activity could take place with adults or peers, and was all the better for plenty of talk, questioning and interruptions! In effect, the adult was crucial in drawing the child forward into new learning, and should not just 'watch and wait'.

Into the present

The second half of the 20th Century saw even more diversity in practice across the world, where different countries took different paths for early learning, often driven by the need to see results from the investment of public money, or the need to support the poorest families, working parents, or those who had been affected by wars and other conflicts.

The Head Start Programme

In the USA, by 2005 the Head Start Programme (established 1965, and expanded by the government in 1981) had reached 22 million pre-school children in deprived areas. It had achieved sufficient benefits to convince the government to invest in its expansion. The programme focuses on families below the poverty line, and particularly emphasises partnership with parents in an attempt to change the life and health of the whole family. Food programmes as well as parent education are central to this project.

Outcomes from research appear to indicate that children are more academically prepared for kindergarten as the result of Head Start pre-schools. However, these same children seemed less socially prepared for the kindergarten experience, and more behavioural problems were noted among the children who came from Head Start pre-schools. The USA government has now established national indicators for learning outcomes, and these emphasise language and social development.

The initiative continues with the support of government, and 'I am Moving, I am Learning' is a recent Head Start initiative, which attempts to reduce childhood obesity by increasing active movement in Head Start settings and in the home. Head Start centres

Head Start: links with home; involvement of parents; nutrition and the healthy family; active and outdoor experiences.

concentrate on providing an environment for the whole family, and in parent education as well as childcare, where play, outdoor experiences and active learning are central.

The High/Scope system

In Ypsilanti, Michigan in the 1960s, a group of teachers led by David Weikart became interested in developing a system for under fives education that combined the work of Piaget, Dewey, and particularly Vygotsky. The High/Scope system, developed in the 1960s as the Perry Pre-school Project, was based in continuing research and focused on supporting children in the poorest families. The High/Scope programme has been monitored since its first days, and results are impressive, looked at both from a government and a child development perspective. After 40 years, the research confirms that for every dollar spent on the programme there is a 16-dollar return to society from such benefits as lower crime, higher employment rates, better social relationships and fewer teenage pregnancies among the adults who had experienced the programme.

High/Scope methods promote active learning in a predictable programme for the day, which includes plan-do-review, small- and large-group times, outside time, transition times, eating and resting times. This system enables children to be confident and secure, and to engage in independent learning, planning their own activities for part of the day, looking back on what they have done and reviewing their own work, and sharing control with the adults as partners in learning.

The High/Scope method also reinforces the notion of 'interest areas' such as blocks, home play, creative play and outdoor play, reminiscent of Montessori's rooms in her 'Children's Houses'. These areas, and the underlying curriculum content of the provision, help children's thinking and planning, and support the teachers in managing the programme. Adults in High/Scope settings are partners and guides, observing, providing and supporting children in developing their interests, and in moving into Vygotsky's 'zone of proximal development'.

High/Scope: activity areas with free access; independent and free choice learning; outdoor play; teacher as observer and scaffold.

Early Years provision in the USA continues to be very varied, as each state (and sometimes each community within a state) has its own Education Board, with tremendous freedom to adapt provision, access national programmes or prescribe curriculum content and organisation. The Kindergarten year, although not a universal funded period, is so familiar that it often occupies permanent provision within state primary schools.

European developments

In Europe there were many and diverse responses to the effects of the Second World War and economic pressures of the time. Reggio Emilia schools were established in Northern Italy to meet the needs of single working mothers, widowed in the Second World War. The system has become respected world-wide and is continuing to expand alongside a more formal state system in Italy, and in Reggio-style schools across the world.

In France, a nation-wide network of Ecoles Maternelles expanded and is now universal throughout France. Germany and Spain also restructured provision for early education during the last half of the 20th Century, either as state-only or state-supported provision. All Scandinavian countries have improved provision, some building on excellent existing practice, others modelled on neighbouring countries. Much of the Scandinavian practice echoes the Froebelian principle of outdoor learning, and many children spend large parts of their day out of doors in all weathers. Other countries, including the UK have taken models of good practice in Scandinavia to improve outdoor provision.

New Zealand and Australia

The Te Whariki early years curriculum was implemented in 1996 in New Zealand, and in Australia, *The Early Years Learning Framework Australia* was developed and eventually implemented in 2009. Both systems have a strong link with Frobelian and Montessori principles, with practice enshrining free play and access to an outside environment. The New Zealand model also makes a strong commitment to the involvement of families and the preservation of native languages.

The Far East

In Japan, China and other far eastern countries, responsibility for pre-school provision is shared between the government and private providers. There is a new and growing pressure from parents for high quality early years provision throughout the Far East, emerging from the increasing prosperity of these countries, and some recent developments in China have produced childcare provision on an industrial scale.

Russia

In Russia, however, the pre- and post-war explosion of early years education, building on both Montessori and Vygotsky, sadly lost impetus after the break-up of the Soviet Union in the 1960s to 1980s, when more than half of the pre-schools collapsed due to lack of funding, Russian early years education, from a principled high point between the wars, has become a very poor relation in the 21st Century.

India

In India, Ghandi committed himself to the concept of universal early years education, and this was fuelled by a visit to India of Maria Montessori in 1939. However, the economic and social conditions in India, as in sub-Saharan Africa, provide constant and enduring problems for governments as they struggle to increase provision in rapidly growing populations.

There is worldwide acceptance of the principles of early years, but different responses according to national wealth, politics and populations. Most providers would uphold the principles of Froebel and Montessori.

The United Kingdom

In the United Kingdom, post-war financial pressures limited the expansion of early education, which continued to be a 'multiple-option' provision, with the emphasis on free choice, play and childcare. Much of the provision was staffed by untrained carers, or parents, and in maintained settings these practitioners were often nursery nurses or care staff whose training had concentrated more on care than on education. Trained nursery teachers were in the minority and usually worked in school-based provision.

The range of settings was huge – from informal childminding and parent and toddler groups; through the Pre-school Playgroup movement where parent volunteers provided play care (sometimes under the direction of a paid leader); to private and state funded nurseries, mostly overseen by Social Services. There were also a small number of Combined Centres providing care and education and state nursery schools and nursery classes in infant or primary schools, generally in deprived inner city areas. There was little interference in the running of these from central government, as parents were thought to be the ones to make decisions about childcare.

The environment and curriculum were the concern of individual settings, and the practitioners within them. They were influenced by the work of Susan Isaacs in establishing high quality nursery provision; the open-air Nursery schools established by the MacMillan Sisters (Rachel and Margaret) in the 1930s; the Montessori and Froebel Institutes; and the Plowden Report, which had a major influence on the practice in early education in 1967. Despite government promises during the 1970s for universal education for all three and four year olds whose parents wanted it, these commitments were shelved due to economic pressures.

UK: where provided, early education in the first half of 20th Century followed long-held principles: open-air; healthy child; active learning/free play and choice; but the quality of provision was unacceptably varied.

The production of substantial evidence of the power of the stimulating environment in reports such as the Rumbold Report *Starting with Quality* (1990) still had little effect on policy makers. It took *Start Right*, the Royal Society of Arts Report (Ball, 1994) to draw real political attention to the situation. This report recommended that high-quality provision should be made available to all three and four year olds, reviewing evidence that high-quality early education leads to lasting cognitive and social benefits in children. Ball set out the following major prerequisites for 'high-quality' provision: an appropriate early learning curriculum; the selection, training, and continuity of staff; high staff/child ratios; buildings and equipment designed for early learning; and a partnership role for parents.

Another recommendation was that the division between education and care should disappear, and that 'edu-care' should be a priority. The report concluded that at the time:

> 'The third lesson from abroad is that Britain is not only on the wrong track, but dangerously ignorant (or complacent) about its situation.'
> *Start Right: The Importance of Early Learning*, Sir Christopher Ball;
> (Royal Society of Arts, 1994).

A strong and continuing reason for this situation was the widely-held view that care and education of young children was mainly a private matter, unless the parents were deemed to have some

'Start Right' Report (1994): recommends universal provision for all three and four year olds in the UK. Suggests a new 'triangle of care' between parents, professionals and community.

disadvantage or disability, and that governments should not intervene. The *Start Right* report suggested a new model in 'The exemplar of the Midwife', a link between health, care and education, bridging the space between families and childcare.

Although both the Rumbold Report and *Start Right* appeared to be shelved by governments after their publication, they did have a lasting influence. In 1996, the national situation changed when reports and research findings combined with the economic need for working mothers, and the government recognised the social and economic benefits of combining early education and care. The result was funding for universal nursery education (for three and four year olds) through government investment. The wide diversity of provision was a big issue, so the Nursery Voucher Scheme was introduced as the route for funding (parents could exchange their vouchers for childcare provision of their choice).

The *Desirable Outcomes for Children's Learning on Entering Compulsory Education* (School Curriculum and Assessment Authority, 1996) provided goals for providers and for effective use of public money. These listed the knowledge, skills and attitudes that children should demonstrate across six areas of learning as they entered school at five. The structure followed the recommendations of government inspectors of the day and linked to the recently implemented National Curriculum for primary schools.

However, the Nursery Vouchers proved unworkable and were abandoned following a change of government. Funding was distributed direct to

settings through the Nursery Education Grant, and the Desirable Outcomes were retained and further refined in 2000 to become the Early Learning Goals for the statutory Foundation Stage Curriculum.

In England, all settings with three to five year olds, including the private, voluntary and independent sectors of provision, were expected to implement this framework, promoting an entitlement for all children to a quality early years environment. However, our old friend, '... poor fidelity of implementation' returns here, and different settings interpreted the framework in very different ways. Some held on to the principles of child-centred practice, others were influenced by downward pressure from later stages of education, and became too formal too early, focusing on teaching, rather than learning.

The new OFSTED inspection system (introduced in the Education Act in September 1992), was not always helpful in giving clear guidance, and in focusing too much on outcomes and less on the process of experiences. Many inspectors and local government advisers in these years of implementation had insufficient experience or knowledge of the early years, and despite copious research, and guidance from such people as Tina Bruce, Kathy Sylva and Audrey Curtis, messages to settings were at best mixed and at worst undermined every early years principle. Conflicting messages about quality became common between the opinions of the local advisory service and OFSTED inspectors.

As provision for under fives expanded, so did provision for under threes, and this resulted in guidance for the age group from birth to three, which was subsequently absorbed into guidance for the full pre-school age range from birth to five (the Early Years Foundation Stage). The roles of Social Services and Education were combined, and Sure Start Children's Centres (modelled on Head Start programmes) began to promote the partnership between professionals and parents.

England: from 2000, national guidance on the elements of curriculum provision was produced in England, including detailed guidance on the indoor and outdoor environments.

Devolution of responsibility for education within the UK has resulted in a difference in both the speed and the detailed character of early education in Wales, Northern Ireland and Scotland. Some are very similar to the developments in England, where there is detailed guidance on the indoor and outdoor environments, others show more influence of Forest School programmes or the work of universities in the different countries. However, these developments all owe allegiance to the great educators of the past – Pestalozzi, Froebel and Maria Montessori.

Free play out of doors continues to be enshrined in the guidance for the early years in most countries.

Their work has resulted in the inclusion (at the heart of the early years curriculum) of the enduring elements of free play, natural materials and outdoor experiences; the involvement of parents and sensitive observation and interaction by practitioners.

The environment

In the early part of the 21st Century, and particularly as many countries of the world find themselves in financial difficulties, the tension between the principles of early education, promoted by specialists, and the economic pressures of producing an educated and socially adept citizenship have re-emerged. The research evidence in support of early learning and quality environments continues to be published throughout the world, and this shows more strongly than ever that future world citizens need to be educated *and* nurtured, and that high quality early intervention can dramatically improve children's chances, if it is conscientiously implemented with child-centred principles.

The history of childcare and education shows quite clearly that the environment is a key player in the early years, and that the way the environment is organised and offered is crucial for parental involvement and children's learning and development. Excellent settings (and there have always been excellent settings) pay close attention to the environment for learning, recognising it as 'The third teacher'.

> 'In order to act as an educator for the child, the environment has to be flexible: it must undergo frequent modification by the children and the teachers in order to remain up-to-date and responsive to their needs to be protagonists in constructing their knowledge.'
> Lella Gandini in *The Hundred Languages of Children*,
> Carolyn Edwards, Lella Gandini and George Forman
> (Ablex Publishing Corporation, 1998).

If we are to be effective in providing quality early learning environments we must be faithful to our beliefs about the way this environment is constructed and maintained.

The Blue and the Green – the environment out of doors

'Every child born in this world has an innate pleasure and delight and interest and curiosity in the natural world.'

David Attenborough

We all have memories of childhood, and many of these will be of being outside, where the sun shone and the days were endless as we collected conkers, waved sticks, jumped ditches, made go-carts and rolled on the grass. The memories of taking risks, getting muddy, eating wild food and being away from adults made the experiences even more exciting and memorable. We would all like the same memories for our own children, where blue and green were the dominant colours, tinged at the edges with mud, bonfire smoke and daisies, and free from the constraints of indoors.

But modern children are different, their priorities are confused with temptations of screen time and a heightened sense of the dangers of being alone out of doors.

> Our own memories should shape our thinking about outdoor areas.

If today's children are to benefit from the same memories we have, then society must take the provision of high quality outdoor experiences seriously, looking carefully at what we provide in settings and schools, which at the moment can consist of *the replacement tree* – a metal climbing frame, never changing, cold and hard; *the fake mud* – concrete or asphalt, hard and unforgiving; *the ready-made* – trikes and scooters, with circular tracks that go nowhere; and *the over-supervision* where adults intervene to remove all risk from the activities.

Outdoor learning

In previous chapters I have explored the contribution of major educational thinkers and practitioners on our curriculum for the early years in the 21st Century. I now wish to explore the vital contribution of the garden or outdoor space to learning in the early years. Froebel coined the description 'kindergarten' as a tribute to his commitment to nature and providing a 'garden for children'.

Others who followed continued and expanded his view of the garden, by enshrining it permanently in the pattern of children's lives, acknowledging the key part played by nature in human development, and replicating the notion of gardens for both work and recreation. Small scale individual gardens in Froebel schools and Montessori's Children's Houses, where children tended vegetables and flowers, were enhanced by a commitment to space for play in fresh air and freedom, with the support of interested adults. Games, songs, and simple play equipment were included in this healthy routine, and we have rightly retained the notion of outdoor play as an essential element of provision today.

The garden for children (the kindergarten) has a long history.

However, we are also at risk of losing this essential part of children's experience as modern living encroaches on our children's lives.

Bronwen Cohen, Guest Editor of Children in Europe, which produced the study *Space to Play, Room to Grow* (2005); and Chief Executive of Children in Scotland, said:

> 'The expansion in services for young children means that they are spending more time in organised child care of some kind.
>
> We are also witnessing a decline in access to safe public space, such as town squares or open countryside. With less freedom to roam and more time spent in organised space it is vitally important that we ensure children have access to the outdoors and the opportunity for freedom to explore. Nature can provide the best environment for a child's play.'
>
> *Curriculum for Excellence* (Scotland, 2010).

So how do we provide a safe, secure and stimulating learning environment out of doors for children in the early years? How do we incorporate all the evidence about learning out of doors, when our lives are increasingly bound to the inside? And how do we provide all those activities from the rosy glow of our own childhoods, the experiences that have made us who we are?

Childhood has changed, and children have far less experience of the natural world.

Health and well-being

Blue and green are important colours for most life forms and it is increasingly apparent that it's not just plants and animals that need to be out of doors, humans need it too. We all need to see the blue sky, to be near green plants, and to feel the effects of sun, weather and the seasons on our skins. A study (2010) at Southampton University Hospital (UK) has found an alarming rise in just a few years in the incidence of rickets, a childhood condition caused by Vitamin D deficiency, which weakens bone structure. Vitamin D is found in oily fish and other fats, but the main source of this vitamin is sunlight.

'In my 22 years at Southampton General Hospital, this is a completely new occurrence in the south that has evolved over the last 12 to 24 months and we are seeing cases across the board, from areas of deprivation up to the middle classes.' Professor Clarke said vitamin D supplements should be more widely adopted to halt the rise in cases. *'There is a real need to get national attention focused on the dangers this presents.'*

He added that the *'…modern lifestyle, which involves a lack of exposure to sunlight, but also covering up in sunshine'* had contributed to the problem. *'The return of rickets in northern parts of the UK came as a surprise, despite the colder climate and lower levels of sunshine in the north, but what has developed in Southampton is quite astonishing,'* said Prof Clarke. *'We are facing the daunting prospect of an area like Southampton, where it is high income, middle class and leafy in its surroundings, seeing increasing numbers of children with rickets, which would have been inconceivable only a year or so ago.'*

Daily Telegraph (12 November, 2010).

Our recent over-use of high factor sunscreens, keeping children indoors when the sun is shining, changes in diet and an increasingly indoor lifestyle seem to have conspired to make our children vulnerable to a condition last seen in Victorian times, and thought to have been eradicated in most cultures many years ago.

'The use of greenspace or 'green exercise' improves health. In particular, learning outdoors generally results in increased levels of physical activity. In addition, interacting with greenspace (walking, gardening, etc) improves emotional wellbeing and mental health.'
Curriculum for Excellence Through Outdoor Learning (Learning and Teaching Scotland, 2010).

New evidence underlines our knowledge that the predominant colours of green and blue found out of doors are not just pleasing to the eye of the painter or the naturalist, they affect us all. Our feelings and moods, our health and even our ability to recover from illness and injury are now known to be affected by exposure to nature. Patients in hospitals with views over gardens get better more quickly, both from physical and mental illnesses, needing fewer drugs and less time for recuperation. Even prisoners have better heath and calmer behaviour if they can see or, even better, work in green spaces and gardens.

> 'An increasing body of research indicates that contact with natural places supports both physical and mental health, aids social and psychological development by providing outlets for risk-taking and physical energy, reduces stress and anti-social behaviour, facilitates social interactions including team-working and informal sociability, and provides visible and worthwhile achievements.'
>
> Forestry Commission's Offenders and Nature Schemes,
> www.forestresearch.gov.uk/offendersandnature

The feel-good factor of these colours, and the physical changes they bring about in our bodies and brains must help. Looking at blue, and particularly sky blue, releases more calming endorphins in our brains than any other colour, and green has a restful, calming reputation because of its associations with growth and the open air. In combination, these effects seem to be so vital to wellbeing that we should be exposing ourselves, and our children, to them whenever we can.

Declining access to outdoor space

Sadly, in recent years, circumstances have combined to restrict children's access to the outdoors, at just the time when we should be increasing it. The study *Space to Play, Room to Grow* (Children in Europe, 2005) which surveyed regulations on outdoor play space in pre-schools and primary schools, reveals that many countries now have no requirement or even recommendation to ensure that every child attending an early years service has access to the outdoor space they need. Where these regulations do exist, they vary across different types of provision, or are so vague that they have no real meaning.

Entitlement to early years care does not necessarily mean an entitlement to high quality outdoor play.

Experience of the outdoor environment is essential for children's physical and emotional growth and well-being, but our culture is increasingly focused indoors. Families spend weekends at the shopping centre; TV and other media tempt us to the screen; and the increase in anxiety about child safety has restricted children's horizons to the back garden, or worse, to the house itself. Some children rarely go outside, and even the walk to school is now less common.

In a now widely publicised article in the Daily Mail in 2007, the shrinking horizons for children in Sheffield, England were clearly described:

> '*When George Thomas was eight he walked everywhere. It was 1926 and his parents were unable to afford the fare for a tram, let alone the cost of a bike and he regularly walked six miles to his favourite fishing haunt without adult supervision.*
>
> *Fast forward to 2007 and Mr Thomas's eight-year-old great-grandson Edward enjoys none of that freedom. He is driven the few minutes to school, is taken by car to a safe place to ride his bike and can roam no more than 300 yards from home.*
>
> *Even if he wanted to play outdoors, none of his friends strays from their home or garden unsupervised.*
>
> *The contrast between Edward and George's childhoods is highlighted in a report which warns that the mental health of 21st-Century children is at risk because they are missing out on the exposure to the natural world enjoyed by past generations.*'
>
> www.dailymail.co.uk/news/article-462091/
> How-children-lost-right-roam-generations.html

And this situation has not improved. A report called *Every Child Outdoors*, commissioned in the UK by the Royal Society for the Protection of Birds and English Nature updates this influence on children's lives, and adds to our knowledge by relating outdoor experiences to the growing number of children with behaviour disorders:

> '*Outdoor activities in nature appear to improve symptoms of ADHD in children by 30% compared with urban outdoor activities and threefold compared with the indoor environment. All children with ADHD may benefit from more time in contact with nature, greener routes to school and more natural views from their windows.*'
>
> *Every Child Outdoors* (Royal Society for the Protection of Birds/
> English Nature, 2010).

Many children reach our schools and settings without being conscious of the outdoor world, and one six year old, asked recently to describe her journey to school wrote:

1. Get out of my car.
2. Walk into the playground.
3. Put my lunch box in the crate.
4. Hang my coat on the peg.
5. I go in my class.

So, in addition to the inclusion of home-like elements in our early years settings indoors, we need to be aware of the essential contribution that outdoor environments and gardens make to play and learning. Despite its inclusion in guidance for good practice in many countries, and across all major methodologies, our good friend '… poor fidelity of implementation' results in very different interpretations of 'outdoor play' across providers, even in the same city or the same country.

Can the situation improve?

Can our society be assured that we provide this essential ingredient for all children? Does our universal and growing entitlement for 'educare' make a real commitment to outdoor learning? Can we be sure that every child, whatever their age, social background or disability is getting the same quality? Or is there as much difference in provision for our growing children as there is in chicken farming?

At its most simple, the aim for universal education and care systems, albeit implemented in a well-intentioned attempt to improve the life chances of all children, could be in danger of providing hot houses, battery farming for children, calculated and organised to produce a homogenised group of equals, brought up in safe and hygienic conditions by conscientious practitioners, and regularly inspected against national criteria.

Is universal 'educare' putting pressure on services and resulting in unsatisfactory or 'battery-type' provision for some children?

Let's look at some criteria for the raising of chickens in large groups and reflect on what an 'educare' version of each might be. Of course, two of the major needs of chickens (and children) are light and space out of doors, and this need is also enshrined in the guidance for early years care wherever a government funds such provision. Here are three major ways of rearing chickens in large groups:

Battery method

In battery methods, up to 50,000 birds live in windowless sheds. Typical stocking density is 17 birds (34 kg) per sq m. Each bird gets a space equivalent to an A4 sheet of paper. Dim lighting discourages activity, with only one hour per day of total darkness for 40 per cent of a bird's life, just four hours for the remainder. There are no perches or toys, broilers do little but eat.

Barn rearing

These chickens are luckier. Like battery hens, they are reared in sheds but at lower stocking densities – a maximum of 30kg per sq m, equivalent to 1.25 sheets of A4 paper per bird. Lighting is varied to simulate the natural cycle, and six hours of total darkness at night allows birds to rest properly. Minimum light by day is bright enough for birds to be active, and perches, straw bales, and toys encourage pecking and activity.

Free range

These hens are seen to have the best lives. They are housed in sheds or chicken houses, with continuous daytime access to clean pasture, except in adverse weather. Outdoor spaces must by law be 'mainly covered with vegetation' and sheltered by hedges and trees. In the sheds, densities must not exceed 27.5kg per sq m.

Information from 'Pecking order' an article by Andrew Purvis
(*The Guardian* on line, 2006).

Can these descriptions compare in any way to education provision for young children, or am I pursuing some artificial and inappropriate analogy? Humour me for a moment as you read these (perhaps extreme) descriptions of provision for our babies and children when cared for outside their own homes, and with a particular focus on their lack of access to fresh air, daylight and the magical effects of green and blue.

Battery children

These situations are fortunately rare, thanks to the guidance and diligent supervision of governments and practitioners, but they do still exist, and the slippery slope to battery rearing is slippery, particularly in periods of financial restraint or lack of trained staff. The children who attend these settings often come from indoor environments at home, where they rarely go outside, and some of the settings they attend have no adjacent outdoor space with direct access for the children. Some of these settings are in shared accommodation or on several floors with even more restrictions on space and access. Because there is limited or little outdoor play and the associated storage, the settings do not have a very wide range of outdoor resources, particularly those that encourage energetic play and exercise the large muscles.

Practitioners are sometimes less informed about the importance of the outdoor environment, and even when they plan visits or walks to parks and local green spaces, the children are closely supervised and have limited opportunities for free choice of resources or activities. At these times, some children are very active and uncontrolled, they have little apparent knowledge of how to use the space and freedom, or of their own safety. Others seem fearful and unconfident in the outdoor space, often asking to go home or indoors, and are even more miserable if the weather is chilly or damp, as they rarely spend time outdoors. These experiences can turn into stressful times for everyone, discouraging practitioners from repeating the visits.

Barn-reared children

For these children, access to the outdoor area is time-limited and some children must wait until the end of the day for their turn in the garden. Of course, there are many reasons for this model - in some of these settings, many children use the same space, so a timetable has been drawn up to prevent overcrowding and restrict the age range in the area at any one time; in others, the garden has no direct access from the building, making adult supervision difficult; in yet other settings, shift patterns, accommodation on more than one floor, or parental views on children being out of doors are cited as reasons why outdoor play is limited or timetabled.

Good practice in free flow play should not be a lottery for children, where some get exciting environments and long periods of access, while others look enviously out of the window or down the stairs at the forbidden land, waiting for their turn. And when children in these settings do get outside, the activities they are offered are generally less open-ended, as the area is used in turn by children of different ages, and the equipment is selected and set out by the adults at the beginning of each day for all the groups to use. The garden often has a man-made, hard play surface, sometimes with small flowerbeds, fixed climbing equipment, occasional trees and bushes, with paths or paving offering some structure for planned play.

Staff in these settings work hard to make outdoor areas more exciting, but as no-one has overall responsibility for the area, and it is used in turn by different groups, their goodwill is often diluted, and the area can become sterile and lacking in stimulation.

To alleviate the problem of unsuitable outdoor spaces, some settings in this group provide large indoor spaces for play, where children can run and ride wheeled toys, but there is no possibility in these spaces for experiencing the changing features of weather, nature or growing things.

Free range children

These children have free access to the outdoor environment for most of the day, and two, three, four and five year olds often use the same area together. Activities in outdoor areas offer a wide range of flexible experiences for developing skills across the whole curriculum. There is plenty of space, and this includes hard surface and grassy areas, bushes, trees and flowers, covered areas and shelters, seats and sensory experiences such as herb gardens. There are open, sunny places and shady corners.

Activities in the outdoor area include digging, gardening and other 'real life' activities such as weather and wildlife watching, woodwork, den building and the use of open-ended materials. Children can access their own equipment and wheeled toys from a well-stocked storage area, or from indoors. There are places to rest and relax, to be quiet and to observe, as well as to be active and creative.

Outdoor experiences

We would all like our children to have the benefits of the sort of free-range experience described above, but it is not currently an entitlement for all children. Is it even a possibility when providers and settings are so different, and operate in such different locations? We must retain the ideal for every

'Free-range' experiences have advantages and disadvantages.

child, that in their early years they have an outdoor experience that is nearer to the 'free range' end of the spectrum. International good practice emphasises the need for children to be out of doors, and in some countries outdoor experiences take up large parts or even the majority of each day:

> 'Nature and the immediate neighbourhood are important elements of the environment.'
>
> 'Early Childhood Education and Care in Finland':
> Brochures of the Ministry of Social Affairs and Health 2004: No.14
> (Ministry of Social Affairs and Health).

The archetypes of free-range childhood that might spring to mind are the lives of itinerant or nomadic children, travellers and Roma people in Europe, Aborigine people in Australia, Maasai or Tuareg in Africa, Marsh Arabs in Iraq, and other such communities all over the world. When we see these children on television and in photos, playing with plastic bag kites and dusty footballs, with bare feet, bright clothing and smiling eager faces, we could be forgiven for envying their freedom. These children appear to have an idyllic life, free from constraints and full of playful experiences with natural, real-life resources, with their parents nearby as models. But, of course, life as a child in a nomadic community is far from idyllic: cold, often hungry, insecure and with associated responsibilities and pressures beyond anything our children could dream of. So let's look nearer to our organised western experiences – what might free-range life look like in a European village?

This example is from rural Greece:

> On the eastern coast of the Peloponnese, just before the coast road ends and turns inland towards Sparta, leaving the deep blue sea, and heading into the green hills of the hinterland, there is a tiny beach village, not much more than a few houses and tavernas clustered round a small but deep harbour. Behind the village and its tomato and aubergine fields rise the steep flanks of the Parnon Mountains – dry, stony, full of scratching cicadas, rocky caves, isolated monasteries and wandering herds of goats.
>
> In this village is the Beach House, an informal community day care centre, perched on a low concrete platform left over from a previous loading bay for tomato boxes. The Beach House is safely enclosed by wire mesh fencing, inside which sits a small house, about five square metres of sandy soil and two trees – a huge pine tree which spreads branches across the whole site – and a tall elegant, whispering

eucalyptus. Both are full of birds and insects, and both regularly drop small surprises of cones, leaves and needles.

The Beach House occupies about a fifth of the remaining space – a single storey building with a wide, shady (if rather ramshackle) veranda with an even more ramshackle awning of faded canvas. The house has one door and one window. The door is always open, although a curtain is often used to deter insects, and in front of the window stands a large table, covered by a plastic cloth, decorated by a large basil plant in a pot, and surrounded by a motley collection of benches, chairs and stools. As well as being used for meals, the benches also serve as beds for siestas for adults and children. A plastic picnic table and chairs are used flexibly to augment space or make another eating area. Sometimes this table is near the front fence so the comings and goings on the beach path and the beach beyond can be studied, or it serves as a base for simple games with cones and other natural materials.

A travel cot has been placed under the pine tree, providing a makeshift playpen where babies can sleep or sit to play or just watch. Wheeled toys of all sorts and conditions are available in abundance, along with household items such as brooms, buckets, dustpans. A garden hose is permanently connected for cooling showers and informal water play, and lines strung from the tree branches are decorated with hats, clothing and swimming costumes. A big insulated water bottle hangs just outside the door, where children can help themselves or indicate a need for a drink.

Into this setting each morning come children – a slightly different group every day, as they are mostly the children of the tourist industry – waiters, cleaners, cooks and kitchen helpers, mostly women, mostly poorly paid, and mostly employed only during the summer. These parents leave their children here every day, in full view of the village, where everyone can see what goes on.

As they go about their daily business, familiar people greet the children through the chain link fence, stopping for a chat and sometimes passing fruit or sweets through the gaps. The carers are led by a large elderly woman dressed totally in black, who spends most of her time sitting at the front of the house, often with a baby or toddler on her knee. She keeps order, arbitrates in disputes, nags the teenage girls who help with the more active aspects of care, and watches over the whole scene, a permanent feature for the whole village, not just the children. Her helpers are local girls, some of whom will continue their role by

training as teachers or becoming childcare workers themselves. The Beach House offers an ideal holiday job for these girls, poorly paid, but near the action of the beach, where they will all spend the evening once their small charges have gone home, and offering a real alternative to taverna work or cleaning villas in the local town.

The day in the Beach House has a predictable pattern – early arrival, plenty of free play in the outside area, a stop for a snack or drink every so often, lunch at the big table under the tree, with the carers and various other adults, including casual visitors from the community, a long siesta (either on one of the benches, on a shady mattress or in a home-made hammock strung in the tree), then more play and a snack before parents or other family members return to collect them. Children play with found materials, either those that fall from the trees or those they find in the garden – a broken chair becomes a castle or a throne; a stick becomes a gun or a magic wand; leaves, cones and stones become pretend food, treasure or money; a toy TV character brought from home becomes a centre of play as the children make a tent and a parachute for him, flying him around the garden and throwing him up to use the parachute, till he eventually gets stuck in the pine tree.

Some of the children also spend time just watching, either the people, traffic and animals going past outside the fence, or each other. In this environment disagreement is rare, there is no need to shout, playthings are plentiful and multi-purpose, adults are always around to help or join in the play. The pace is leisurely, particularly in the evening, when family members stay for a chat before taking their children to one of the beach bars for ice cream or chips before returning home.

The children in the 'Beach House' appear to have a truly free-range provision, with necessities provided and maximum freedom, minimum constraint.

We all want our children to have the freedom and excitement we remember from our own childhoods, with the glow that distance lends! We want them to have the best of both worlds, the freedom of our own childhoods plus the benefits of the modern world. Richard Louv, in his thought-provoking and inspiring book *The Last Child in the Woods*, describes the experiences he had as a child, and the way these have been eroded for his own children, making them anxious and even fearful of simple outdoor activities:

'A kid today can likely tell you about the Amazon rainforest – but not about the last time he or she explored the woods in solitude, or lay in a field listening to the wind and watching the clouds move ... For a new generation, nature is more abstraction than reality. Increasingly, nature is something to watch, to consume, to wear – to ignore.'
The Last Child in the Woods, Richard Louv (Algonquin, 2008).

Just as we are becoming more informed about the influence of the natural world (a crucial element in our children's well-being, not just during childhood, but for the whole of their lives), experience of a 'learning garden' is in danger of becoming a rarity for some children, a casualty of our modern world and our new priorities.

The ideals of outdoor provision

So if we accept that children benefit from being out of doors, what are the ideals for provision that we should aspire to? Of course, these need to be adapted to different circumstances, but access to the benefits of 'the blue and the green' should not be a lottery for children, with some early lives being far richer than others. We know that the architecture of the brain is massively influenced by experiences before the age of five or six, so we should make sure that the experiences in our pre-schools, nurseries and schools are as **Key elements when planning and resourcing outdoor environments.** rich as possible, and include frequent opportunities to learn out of doors. This essential building block for future health and happiness should be available to every child equally.

Key elements for successful outdoor experiences will include:

- freedom
- space to do things on a bigger scale than indoors
- open-ended materials
- natural objects
- friends.

It is useful to have a structure to help our thinking when we look at our own provision. Jim Greenman, in his book *Caring Spaces, Learning Places* (Exchange Press, 2005), has a very useful checklist for reflecting on your current outdoor learning space, and I have used it as the basis for the following list.

Outdoor spaces should include the following:

Places for active motor play, including:	Places to be human, including places to:	Places to be creative and construct, to:	Environmental places where children can:
• swinging • sliding, rolling • climbing • jumping • running • bouncing • balancing • travelling • riding • transporting • moving slowly	• watch • wonder • retreat • sleep • eat • shelter, lean, sit and lie • discover • experience different views, weathers, micro-climates	• build • explore machines • pretend • create • make music • express yourself • pretend	• dig • grow, tend and harvest • explore watery places • watch bird, animal and insect life • collect and carry natural objects • measure and count • experience weather and climate • feel sheltered
	Places to be an adult		
	• watching • responding • interacting • joining in		

Jim Greenman also includes a reference in his book to Nicholson's 'Theory of Loose Parts', an exploration of the place of open-ended materials in children's play, both indoors and outside:

> *'Kids really get to know the environment if they can dig it, beat it, swat it, lift it, push it, join it, combine different things with it. This is what adults call creative activity, it is what artists do... a process of imagination and environment working together.'*
>
> *Caring Spaces, Learning Places,* Jim Greenman
> (Exchange Press, 2005).

Nicholson maintains that a field has thousands of these 'loose parts' – a television has none. Children's play and learning will be vastly enhanced if both the indoor and particularly the outdoor environments, especially the garden, are full of 'loose parts' – guttering, drain-pipes, logs, planks, clips, pegs, rope, sheets, string, tape, wire, sand, water, mud, stones, sticks, leaves, bags, boxes – and the time and permission to explore them.

In Chapter 5 of this book, you will find some ideas for the resources that can provide rich learning for babies and children in care settings and the early years of school. I have used Jim Greenman's taxonomy when suggesting and organising these resources.

'Spaces that have four walls like the classrooms in many of our schools are not what is required. Why do children seek out the untidy or incomplete, ruined buildings or building sites? Buildings that offer young children the chance to re-order, complete or knock down like sandcastles on a beach, provide their brains with room to grow and mature.

The freedom and space that nature offers can provide inspiration for designing indoor spaces too. When we observe children's behaviour in this natural environment we can see them observing every small detail and absorbing everything around them. In nature they find a reflection of their own world.'

Matti Bergstrom, Emeritus Professor of Neurophysiology at the University of Helsinki, in 'Children in Europe' (2005).

Science, history and our own experience tell us loud and clear that a high-quality learning environment is essential to mental and physical health, and to building brains through experience of all the wonders of the natural world. In our stressful world, we would do well to remember that:

'...the findings of over one hundred studies confirm that one of the main benefits of spending time in nature is stress reduction.'

Last Child in the Woods, Richard Louv (Algonquin, 2008).

A garden for learning

So what do children need to be successful learners out of doors? What are the characteristics of a 'learning garden'?

After many years in education, watching children at play and at work, and reading the works of many eminent educational 'movers and shakers', I now believe that the most successful outdoor places for children resemble gardens more than classrooms or playgrounds. And what do we all do in gardens? We grow things, we dig and build structures, we make ponds and water features, watch birds and other animals. We relax with our families and friends, we cook, eat, drink, have parties, draw, write and read, listen to the radio, watch the weather and experience the seasons. In fact, given time and some good weather, many of us would live out of doors for much of our time. Think of your favourite gardens, or parts of your own garden. Why do you like these places? What makes them so special for you? Why are gardening and garden design books and programmes so popular?

Children will use an early years garden for all these purposes too. In fact, they will be even more active and adventurous in a garden, adding to all the reflective and controlled occupations of adults by climbing, jumping, running, splashing, riding, swinging and shouting, and as they play, they will explore every area of the curriculum, with the added benefits of space, scale and freedom.

Here are six key aspects, which may shed a new light on your setting, and as you read each one, reflect on your own early years garden, its strengths and the ways you could improve the provision for the children you work with. Think about the spaces and activities that children enjoy most, and consider how you might improve those where the magic is missing. Has your garden been affected by too much adult direction or too little; too much attention to tidiness or a lack of care and attention; too much man-made equipment and not enough 'loose parts' for independent and creative learning?

In a garden for learning children need:

- places
- purposes
- people
- personalisation
- playfulness
- peace.

Places

A learning garden isn't one place, it can be hundreds of different places on different days, for different children and adults. Places in the garden need to suit different weathers and seasons, different moods and activities, different interests and childhood passions. Some places in the garden will be sheltered and quiet, others offer space for boisterous play, running, jumping and chasing. There will be places for riding, pulling and pushing vehicles, taking babies for walks, and role-play involving rescuing people from fires or other dangers. There will be places for climbing, for being high up and looking down on your world, for hiding and peeking out, for digging and for just watching. Even the smallest garden can provide corners and zones for both boisterous and quiet play.

Flexible places, resources and adults can adapt to the moods of different days and different children. A garden can provide the space for a pirate island, a parade, a fairy glen, a bear hunt, or an impromptu picnic. Individual children and groups of friends can construct a den or a castle on the top of the climbing frame, which immediately becomes the centre of interest for the whole group. The blooming of the first bulbs planted in the autumn inspires photography and outdoor drawing. A plastic carrier-bag blown in from the street sets off a flurry of kite-making on a windy day. Or the need for shade in a heat wave prompts adults and children to work together to solve the problem of providing shade for a story.

And, of course, different days have different demands. A windy day will require more space for running, a hot summer afternoon will require shade, snowy and frosty days will need shelter, and the ever present risk of rain means that gardens need gazebos, sheltered verandas or plenty of waterproofs and umbrellas! An inspiring garden will encourage constructive and creative play, not just what one practitioner described as 'boys batting around on bikes while the adults huddle and shiver'.

Purposes

If the garden is to provide for every child's purposes, then it must be flexible and open to adaptation. Materials and equipment should be easily moved (preferably by the children themselves as they get older) to meet the daily preoccupations of the group. Outdoor role-play areas are better if they take place in dens and tents; wheeled toys benefit more from the provision of playground chalk than ready-painted lines that always go to the same places. Those 'loose parts', which for outdoor learning also include crates, guttering, rope, drainpipes, fabrics and boxes should be easily accessed and constructed by children, whether this is to provide the structure for a waterway; a picnic of natural materials carefully played out on leaves and stones; a new or extended den; a partition to provide a more private area for role-play or the roadway to a forest.

Gardens that have huge, fixed climbing frames taking up valuable space can restrict creativity, unless adults use their imagination to adapt such frames, adding a curtain track for shower curtains, pulleys and buckets, platforms, walkie-talkies, binoculars, flagpoles and chutes. Large, flat-paved or Tarmac areas can limit play unless simple screens, cones or roped areas are provided where seating, pop-up tents or other shelters, and ground-based play areas can be safely constructed by children to protect their quieter play. Shared areas can become sterile unless inventive adults are determined to make them both accessible and inviting by providing resources on trolleys, in boxes, bags or baskets, to make learning possible in what might otherwise lack inspiration.

Another way to help with personalisation is to think about the surfaces in your garden – hard surfaces such as paving, Tarmac or metal, textured surfaces such as sand and gravel, natural, softer surfaces such as grass, bark, wood and rubber – these can all have a place in your setting, and each will provide a different experience for hands, feet or wheels. Some surfaces feel warm, others are very cold, some invite sitting and lying down, others provide bounce for a ball and purchase for running feet. These permanent surfaces (whether horizontal or vertical, such as shed walls, fences or railings) can also be adapted by adding fabrics, carpet pieces, sheets, netting, cushions, bean bags, small chairs, picnic tables, log slices or cork tiles.

Imaginative practitioners open their minds to the wide range of possibilities and purposes provided by their own learning gardens. They resist the temptation to think that a small or difficult space, a non-existent budget, or over-anxious parents means an inevitable limit on the purposes they can provide. They rise above these problems and work together to provide an exciting environment on a shoestring, often with help from parents, community members, or the children themselves.

People

Children need other people, and of course, top of their list for play partners will usually be other children, their friends, who will engage enthusiastically in play that is great fun, but also leads to extended learning. Children need both time and space for outdoor play, and practitioners should avoid planning adult-directed activities during free-flow periods when children have access to the garden. During such free-flow sessions all the children should be available as play partners and so should all the adults, providing all children in the group with a real choice of where, what and who they choose to play with.

It has been said that there is no such thing as unsuitable weather for outdoor play, just unwilling adults, and in a learning garden, adults need places to perch or to sit as they look, talk and play with children. The scale of a children's learning garden will be child-scale, but this must not exclude adults from their essential part in scaffolding learning and engaging in the magic of sustained shared thinking. Adults need to be able to draw up a chair of a suitable height, to sit beside a child on a bench or seat, or to bring an activity to a comfortable shared surface.

Children will often invite an adult to join their play, or will ask them to provide help or additional resources to support the extension of their activities, but they will only do this if the adults are visibly available and interested in what the children are doing. Practitioners who do not enjoy being outside, or who give children the impression that they are only present to ensure safety and supervision, should consider the messages they are giving to children through their body language, attitude and language. Children need enthusiastic adult support in outdoor play if the play is to progress beyond just exercise and become real learning. These adult play partners will be sensitive to children's needs and will join them in their play without taking over. They observe children's current interests and follow these up by providing additional ideas and resources, offering these so they become an extension of the child's play, not interference by the adult.

Personalisation

Children should spend time outside every day, in both free and planned activities, and parents must be made aware of the reasons why this experience is so important for young children, and the value of outdoor play to learning, particularly for the more active and energetic children. But these are not the only ones who need a garden! Quieter, more reflective children also have a right to learn out of doors, to sit quietly, to build, read, create and perform on a smaller scale, in places that are protected from the more energetic play of the most boisterous.

A garden should provide opportunities for personalisation. Children need to make it their own. Marks and structures define us. Think of the ways we design our own gardens, digging flower beds, making deck areas and water features, planting hanging baskets or window boxes, erecting gazebos and summer houses – even the allotment shed or the designer roof garden. In England alone there are hundreds of thousands of gardens and every one is different! We personalise our outdoor spaces to complement our homes, making the space our own, controlling nature to our own designs, and children need to do the same.

In order to make learning real and permanent, babies and children need to feel both relaxed and in control. Whether this involves lying under a tree, watching the leaves in the breeze, making marks on the paving, weaving ribbons into the fence, making a new den from boxes and other found materials, laying out pebbles and shells brought out from indoors in a pattern, planting seeds and watching them grow, making a bed for a favourite teddy, testing physical strength, skill and speed, or just hanging out in a special corner with a friend or a key person – personalising the space brings it into children's control and enables them to engage with it more deeply. Personalising space should be a priority for us in the gardens we provide.

Children need easy access to a range of resources for personalising spaces – mats, boxes, screens, rugs, playground chalk, baskets and other containers, and of course, all those loose parts described earlier in this chapter.

Playfulness

The garden should be a place of fun. It is easy to become distracted by the constraints of the curriculum, trying to shoehorn activities into this area or that, and forgetting that the enjoyment of being out of doors is an objective in itself! The early years garden should be a place of surprises and discoveries – a spider's web, a new flower on the nasturtiums, the ripening tomatoes, a butterfly, the ice on a puddle, the trail made by a plane in the sky or simply the wind in your hair.

Adults should contribute to the sense of fun and surprise, including laying 'traps' for learning, which is fun for the trapper as well as the children who find them! An object such as a puppet or soft toy in an unusual pace, a

familiar activity such as drinks or snacks presented in a new way out of doors, a piece of equipment missing or in a different place, or a locked shed with no key can provide an opportunity for fun, problem solving and a new direction in the play.

Learning gardens need to have a 'work in progress' feel and look – nothing too perfect, not too tidy, sometimes bedecked with home-made bunting or amateur shelters, with labels and notices written by children, but with a sense of joy in experiment, creation and construction. These gardens should be full of the buzz of communication and the sound of laughter, which are the engines of successful learning.

Peace

Even in the most exciting gardens, there should be a sense of peace. As adults we often seek the 'blue and the green' when we feel stressed or need time to think or cope with difficulties. Children need this sense of respite too, and every garden should offer places for peace and reflection. This could be a sensory flowerbed with a little bench, a quiet corner with a tarpaulin roof, a shady seat under a tree, or a big cardboard box with a net curtain over the opening for a door.

As you look at your learning garden, think about quiet places where babies and children can rest and retreat from what is often a very busy schedule. In bigger settings with more space, planting and permanent structures can help with this planning, but even in the smallest gardens, screens, fabrics and tents can provide a sense of security and privacy. Wind chimes, ribbons and streamers, perfumed flowers and plants in tubs or pots, simple seating such as children's deckchairs, boxes of natural materials, soft toys and books, even a portable CD player can help to offer a place to talk and rest. Storage is essential, and this should ideally be accessible to the children, so they can select, get out and return equipment themselves. Some storage can be mobile, on trolleys or boxes with wheels.

The structure of a garden

The structure of any garden should provide open space for active play such as running and playing with balls. There should also be areas where children can:

- ride bikes and wheeled toys
- observe and experience nature by digging, gardening, and caring for plants, insects and animals
- climb, construct and build dens
- be creative, with painting and mark making
- be quiet and reflective.

In this way we will be able to meet the needs of every child, every day, in any weather, and respond sensitively to their learning as we join them in their play, rather than, as Jean Piaget wrote:

The Blue and the Green

'Time outdoors is another gift that teachers can share with children. It is easy to say that time outside should be as rich and meaningful as time spent in the classroom, but this is not often the case. Many teachers are afraid to let children stay outside on a beautiful day because they fear it will be perceived as 'doing nothing.'

Theories of Childhood, Carol Garhart Mooney
(Redleaf Press, 2000).

Your learning garden is one of the most important places for learning, and *the* favourite place of many children!

As you continue to read this book and reflect on your own practice, remember that the outside world is of equal importance to the inside of your setting. It should take up as much space in your professional commitment as the indoor world.

Attachment and attunement – what do babies and toddlers need?

This chapter attempts to outline the key elements of a caring environment for the youngest children, those from birth until they are about two and a half. It covers the stage of very rapid growth from the newborn, totally dependent on their parents and carers for every need, to the so-called Terrible Twos, tearing themselves away from adult influence with 'Leave me! I can do it myself!'

Attachment and attunement

Babies and toddlers need two things. They need to feel *attached* to the people who care for them – their parents and their principal carers in day care, and they need to know that the adults they are attached to are *attuned* to them. This focus on attachment and attunement should be the guide to relationships, and it must also permeate the environment we provide for babies and toddlers. High quality provision can and does take place in

Babies and toddlers need both attachment and attunement (responsive care).

settings where the resources are sparse, the building is not ideal, and the outside area belongs to the community, but the quality of the relationships is such that babies and children thrive, and parents know that they are valued.

Attachment is vital for babies and children, and the quality of their feelings of secure attachment will affect their entire lives, because securely attached children become securely attached adults. A securely attached baby or toddler is one who may show distress when their parent or major carer leaves them *but* they can cope with this distress and it doesn't last for an unreasonable length of time. Children who are less securely attached will react at the unreasonable ends of behaviour. Some may become extremely distressed, resistant to any comforting, and will remain distressed for long periods. They often become very distressed again when their parent or carer returns, almost as if they were punishing the carer for leaving them. Other less securely attached children show no sign of distress when the major caregiver leaves, and no sign of either pleasure or distress on their return. Fortunately, children in these last two groups are in the minority, with research in 1998 indicating that insecure attachment is present in only seven to fifteen per cent of children.

How experiences affect brain development

However, we do now know that:

> 'Critical aspects of brain architecture begin to be shaped by experience before and soon after birth, and many fundamental aspects of that architecture are established well before a child enters school.
>
> That is to say, the quality of a child's early environment and the availability of appropriate experiences at the right stages of development are crucial in determining the strength or weakness of the brain's architecture, which, in turn, determines how well he or she will be able to think and to regulate emotions. Once established, a weak foundation can have detrimental effects on further brain development, even if a healthy environment is restored at a later age.
>
> The environment of relationships in which young children live literally shapes the architecture of their brains. Effective programs provide center-based, growth-promoting experiences for the children, as well as help their parents create a home environment that provides the kind of positive social interactions, rich language exposure, and early literacy experiences that increase the probability that their child will enter school with the social, emotional, and cognitive skills needed to succeed.'
>
> 'The Timing and Quality of Early Years Experiences Combine to Shape Brain Architecture': Working Paper 5, National Scientific Council on the Developing Child, (Harvard University, 2008).

Once more, in this paper from Harvard, we are reminded of the importance of early experiences on the construction of children's 'brain architecture' and the long-lasting effects of a weak or stressful environment. The Harvard paper also stresses the vital part played by relationships between children and their carers, both at home and in care settings.

Brain development before birth

In order to understand what babies are like, and what they need, we should start before birth, as it is clear that learning does not begin when a baby is born but long before, as babies start the lifetime job of brain building. At birth, babies' brains are not the 'blank slates' we once thought – many of the thousands of millions of cells (neurons) in babies' brains are already 'hard wired' for automatic response, and these include the instructions for staying alive, such as breathing, sucking, blinking and crying. Crying is the way babies communicate, and babies produce different cries that mean different things, with the vocal mechanism hard wired, and the tone and volume learned through early experience. If we had to teach babies to cry, they would be in danger of death from hunger, cold or thirst while they learned!

Recently acquired knowledge about brain development has influenced guidance on parenting, and on early years care, emphasising the time before birth as just as important as the early years between birth and five:

The first *six* years of a child's life, including the year before birth are the most important.

> '*The most important six years in a person's life are up to the age of five.*'
> *How Small Children Make a Big Difference*, Alan Sinclair
> (The Work Foundation, 2007).

The latest national guidance on care for very young children in Scotland recognises that learning doesn't start at birth, but before – the guidance is entitled *Pre-Birth to Three: Positive Outcomes for Scotland's Children and their Families* and includes this commitment:

> *The period between pregnancy and 3 years is increasingly seen as a critical period in shaping children's life chances, based on evidence of brain formation, communication and language development, and the impact of relationships formed during this period on mental health. It is therefore also a critical opportunity to intervene and break cycles of poor outcomes.*
> *Pre-Birth to Three: Positive outcomes for Scotland's Children and their Families* (Learning and Teaching Scotland, 2010).

Before birth, the baby is already working on linking brain cells, but of course, the stimulation received in the womb becomes as nothing compared to life outside the womb. As soon as the baby is born, the number of connections between brain cells explodes. This number will become vastly greater than the baby will need, but enables them to explore and select the best route from multiple pathways. Each time the baby makes a movement, learns to do something, begins to recognise a familiar face, voice or toy, or finds out that they can make things happen by crying, the favoured route between neurons is reinforced and the practice begins to make perfect! Think of the wonderful day when a baby first smiles, usually by accident, certainly not on purpose. But the response from adults is dramatic, and their delight will stimulate the baby to struggle until they get those muscles together again and repeat the process, practising again and again, even on soft toys and photographs, until they can smile at will.

This essential early brain building, and the provision of stimulating early years experiences was, until relatively recently, the sole responsibility of parents, sometimes with the help of the wider family and maybe a health visitor. Again, our attention is drawn to the very different experiences of 21st Century babies and children to those in the past. Many babies attend out of home childcare settings from their **Stable relationships are at the heart of high quality care.** earliest days, and are cared for during most of their waking hours by people who are not their parents. This can raise tensions for the baby and for the adults, and we now know that stress of any sort triggers chemicals in the brain that can damage the links between brain cells, undermining even hard-wired confidence and ability.

Hard-wiring

Other, hard-wired at birth, and permanent connections help babies to recognise the human face, keep themselves warm when we take off all their clothes, sleep (mostly) when they are tired, and concentrate on things that interest them, in particular the human face and voice. This 'hard-wiring' is automatic for the vast majority of babies, although not all. Babies and children with autism appear to have difficulty relating to human faces and voices and understanding the importance of these. Some babies take longer to latch on to breast-feeding while others need help with the start-up pattern of breathing or circulation. Most babies, however, are able to engage with their environment from birth, turning their head to the sound of their mother's voice and breathing, feeding, crying and watching the world on an internal automatic pilot.

Babies have human faces 'hard-wired' in their brains, and adults have babies 'hard-wired' too. This feeling of being connected to a baby as they give you that 'hard look' stare of interest is a trigger, switching on our reciprocal interest in them. When we see or hold a baby, we automatically hold them close to us, so their immature vision can focus on us or the objects we offer them, we talk in that singsong, high pitched way that babies can hear best, and, because we know that a stimulating environment will engage even the youngest of babies, we behave in an animated way when we are with them. In this way, through attunement, or responsive care, we use our knowledge of the world to help them in their explorations, because as well as hard-wired connections, babies' brains also contain 'soft-wiring'.

Soft-wiring

Soft-wiring consists of links between brain cells that have not yet been practised enough to be covered in myelin, a fatty coating that helps to make connections permanent, or hard-wired. The almost miraculous myelin coating is laid down on neural connections by practice and experience, by watching, listening, doing, and particularly by practice. Every time a baby (or any human being) repeats or revisits a concept or skill, the best route for that skill will be consolidated, and the protective coating of myelin becomes thicker, protecting the pathway and making the skill or knowledge easier and faster to recall.

This process of soft-wiring happens at an amazing rate, building up a complex map, affected by every experience the baby has ever had. For example, even before birth, the diet their mother had during pregnancy, the sort of foods she liked, affected this map of soft-wiring. Soft-wiring of relationships and language has been built as the baby listened to the voices they heard in the womb – if they heard loud voices and strident tones, and felt the effects of associated stress chemicals through the umbilical cord, this may well affect the way they develop hearing and speech, and more importantly, the way they respond to  voices after birth. After birth, babies learn all the time, and by practice improve their skills of communication, muscle management and even the focus of their eyes. Babies need to practise looking in order to get better at it.

We can switch the soft-wiring or the myelin off by the way we respond to the child – if we don't make eye-contact with a baby, they will become distressed, if we speak harshly to a toddler, they will produce stress hormones that destroy the very myelin we are trying to build. Raised voices, rough handling, lack of respect and sudden changes have no place in an early years setting.

And there is yet more! Alison Gopnik in her book *The Philosophical Baby* draws together the most recent research into babies and how they think, and the conclusions she comes to are profound, making us question many of our previous assumptions about the behaviour of very young children:

> *We used to think that babies and young children were irrational, egocentric and amoral. Their thinking and experience were concrete, immediate, and limited. In fact psychologists and neuroscientists have discovered that babies not only learn more, but imagine more, care more, and experience more than we would ever have thought possible.*
>
> The Philosophical Baby, Alison Gopnik (Bodley Head, 2009).

This wonderful book offers a picture of the abilities babies and young children have to empathise, problem solve, invent, remember, plan and predict, and possibly to do this in a more creative and imaginative way than adults, whose brains are so much less pliable and creative. Alison Gopnik concludes that the fundamental activity of childhood – play – is truly a way of making sense of the world and children's experiences of it. Role-play is a crucial element in this, as babies and children play out their thoughts, imaginings and experiences; from the eighteen month old brushing her hair with a pen, through the 'what ifs' of tea parties with leaves and stones, to the complex play of junior superheroes, practising what it is like to be grown up, to fly, to rescue people, to change lives. In this way, Alison Gopnik proposes, children are able to explore alternatives, possibilities and new scenarios:

Babies and toddlers can think, invent and imagine.

> '... It's not that two-year-olds pretend because we give them dolls; instead we give them dolls because they love to pretend.'
>
> The Philosophical Baby, Alison Gopnik (Bodley Head, 2009).

Stable relationships

The provision of stable relationships is at the heart of provision for very young children. Everything we do should be built round secure relationships between babies and their main carers (parents and their key person in day care), and other experiences should assume consistent adult presence wherever possible. No activities or routines should replace the loving care of adults, and this is why the ratios in settings for babies must be very favourable, allowing each key adult to know each of their key babies and their family really well. No baby toys or mobiles, no music boxes, comforters or 'blankies' can replace the caring, interested adult:

Defining attachment and attunement (responsive care)

> In an active learning infant-toddler setting, schedules (the daily sequence of events such as choice time, lunch, outside time) and routines (caregiving interactions during eating, napping and bodily care) are anchored for each child around a primary caregiver.
> *Tender Care and Early Learning*, Jacalyn Post and Mary Hohmann (High/Scope Press, 2000).

A combination of security and predictability in the session, with care that meets the needs of the individual, lies at the heart of a high quality environment for babies and toddlers. The essential ingredients for a successful approach are:

Attachment

Babies and young children need to feel attached to the important people, places and comfort objects in their lives, and often find changes between carers difficult. Attachment is a feeling of stability and being known as an individual, with unique needs. In care settings, the key person lies at the heart of attachment, and the concept of this close relationship has resulted in the replacement of the title and role 'key worker' with that of 'key *person*', and the difference between a key worker and a key person has been clarified in the Early Years Foundation Stage guidance (England) in this description:

> 'A key person has special responsibilities for working with a small number of children, giving them the reassurance to feel safe and cared for and building relationships with their parents.'
> *Practice Guidance for the Early Years Foundation Stage* (Department for Education and Skills, 2007).

The effect of a stable attachment with a key person is underlined here:

> 'An infant who has at least one secure attachment will be more likely to develop secure relationships with other people in the world, such as grandparents, other familiar adults and children, and care and educational professionals.'
>
> *Understanding Young Children's Behavior*, Jillian Rodd
> (Teachers College Press, 1996).

Responsive care, or attunement

Babies and young children need people who are not only allocated the responsibility to care for them, but are genuinely interested in them, in their unique needs and their unique families. They do *not* need practitioners or parents who are hurried, unresponsive or distracted. A key person approach is also at the centre of good practice in attunement in childcare, and is underpinned by such activities as pre-admission home visits, managing the settling-in process, making a close relationship with parents and collecting information about likes, dislikes, favourite activities, sleep habits and so on. A well-supported introduction to the care setting becomes responsive care as the key person for each child continues to play a central part in their life. They observe and spend time with the child, building up a picture of their personality, needs and the ways in which they learn, providing a permanent and secure base to their time in the setting:

> 'Attunement is when the adult is able to tune in to babies' needs, perhaps by closely observing their sounds, expressions and body language in a responsive and empathetic way. The important process of attunement begins between mother and baby even before a baby is born.'
>
> *Pre-Birth to Three: Positive Outcomes for Scotland's Children and Families* (Learning and Teaching Scotland, 2010).

A setting where both attachment and attunement are in place is a place of constant communication between adults and children – laughter, games and quiet chats; children and adults asking and answering questions; showing, telling, singing and rhyming fill the air and the day. Adults join the children as play partners, not as directors, watching and waiting before joining the play, and modelling the turn-taking of human conversations. All children are born communicators, and at home there are many times during the day when a parent and child will carry on a conversation, even when the child is a very young baby. Parents, and most practitioners, have a natural instinct to talk to babies, and encourage any sound or movement in response.

Other key needs

What then are the key needs in addition to attachment and attunement?

Key areas of need for babies and toddlers

Predictability and routine – a sense of calm

Babies and young children thrive on routine, but this routine should be flexible enough to meet the needs of individual children. Of course, practitioners could not plan and organise a completely individualised programme for each of the children in their care, in the way that parents can, but it does involve us in seeking and maintaining a balance between the needs of individuals and the smooth running of the setting. A distressed child or a need to finish an activity should not be compromised by the need to have a snack on time!

> 'We have often seen in nurseries a child's 'key worker' attending to impersonal tasks while he was fed or comforted by another member of staff. Unless the key person system is given primacy in the organisation of the day, the child may have no more contact with his designated worker than with any of the other adults. Very small children can only recognise a special interest if it is expressed in close personal interaction day by day.'
>
> People Under Three, Elinor Goldschmeid and Sonia Jackson (Routledge, 1994).

> 'The goal of the daily schedule is to allow individualised care and learning within a smoothly running, predictable day.'
>
> Prime Times, Jim Greenman and Anne Stonehouse (Redleaf Press, 1996).

All children need a calm environment and an un-hurried programme. Their response times are longer than those of adults, and a fast-flowing, noisy nursery environment can be very disorientating for them. Creating a balance, where stimulating activities are presented in a calm, well-ordered and predictable way is not easy, but it is vital.

> 'Good programs slow down to child time. This are done at a child's pace, encouraging and supporting them to undertake activities

themselves as they are ready developmentally, rather than rushing through routines at an efficient adult pace.'

Prime Times, Jim Greenman and Anne Stonehouse (Redleaf Press, 1996).

The ideal setting for babies and toddlers is one where attachment and attunement are carefully balanced, and where routines and relationships support transitions between home and care, between parent and key person, between babies and their carers. This ideal can only be achieved by the most committed, the most skilful, the most flexible, and the most sensitive practitioners – and what do we often do? We staff our baby and toddler rooms with the most inexperienced staff, often without the support of a more practised colleague! It is as though we think that, because these small people can't move very fast or talk, babies and toddlers don't need the most skilful and experienced care. It is a version of the all too common view in society that early childhood care is less important than the school years, which in turn are less important than later schooling or college education, and that such care can be provided on the cheap, with poorly paid practitioners, often working in less than ideal circumstances. It is time that the human race, and particularly those humans who decide on funding for early childhood care and education, take note of the scientific evidence that now clearly tells us of the crucial importance of the early years, not just to successful childhood, but to enriched and useful adulthood.

Adults are an essential resource, and they need to be highly skilled, knowledgeable about child development and committed to becoming attuned to the children in their key group.

The adults as an essential element of the environment

Without good practitioners, the best buildings and resources will fail to provide what babies and young children need, but out-of-home care can also put as much pressure on practitioners as it does on parents and children. Parents are often rushed or tired, many are working, and these pressures can result in guilt, more pressure and inappropriate responses to care staff or even to their own child. Practitioners need to be sensitive to the pressures on parents and try to support them, avoiding critical or negative comments that can just end up in more stress for everyone. The well-being of the child is paramount, and the practitioner's aim should be to preserve the child's sense of self, avoiding conflict wherever possible. The provision of spaces where parents can catch their breath in private before leaving for home can be very helpful.

Adults are important in attachment and attunement, they are an essential resource in the setting and their quality has a direct influence on the quality of provision. Of course there are pressures on practitioners too! Attunement can take a key person too close to a baby or child, clouding her judgement and sometimes even making her resent the presence of the child's parents. Being a replacement carer, particularly in a baby room is a sensitive and difficult task, and is still too often given to the youngest and least experienced members of staff, without the necessary training and professional support.

One practitioner said of her first year in a baby room, 'I had no special training for working with babies, and I began to think that as long as they were wet one end (by regular bottle feeding) and dry the other (by regular nappy changing) then I was doing my job. The rest of the time was spent in routine chores such as washing all the already clean toys, mopping floors or cutting out pictures to stick on the walls. We were discouraged from picking the babies up, because this was thought to make them demanding, and we left babies to cry because we were told that it strengthened their lungs!'

What a change we see in her practice today, as this practitioner manages a very different setting where every new baby has an experienced key person, who also trains and supports younger members of the team in the complex role of working with very young children. Babies are greeted with smiles when they wake, gently lifted from their cots and carried in their key person's arms as the adult talks and sings to them, showing them interesting things and demonstrating how important every baby is.

Babies sit, lie, creep and crawl on the warm and comfortable floor, always with adults nearby to respond to their needs, and join them in their play. Communication with parents is frequent and friendly, every baby is known well by their key person, and parents know who to contact if they are worried, or have information to share. Does this make the babies more demanding and less able to communicate – *no*. These babies are content, communicative and are obviously having a great time; they are well attuned and well cared for, thank goodness their manager didn't give up on learning about their needs!

> 'The teacher's first duty is to watch over the environment, and this takes precedence over all the rest. Its influence is indirect, but unless it be well done there will be no effective and permanent results of any kind, physical, intellectual or spiritual.'
>
> Maria Montessori

The best environments

Once the practitioners in the setting have made a strong bond with parents, through home visits and discussions, as well as the frequent 'doorstep' conversations as the baby passes between their key carers, practitioners embark on the complex task of providing a 'rich and stimulating environment' for babies. Key features of the best environments for babies and toddlers will include a 'home away from home' but suitable for a very big family. This is the ideal for a setting for babies and toddlers. It should be more like a home than a school, more domestic than institutional, and should include furniture and equipment that Maria Montessori would recognise – real furniture and equipment, but child sized, reflecting the lives of real people, and the activities familiar in children's own homes. This principle should pervade all parts of the setting, even those for babies, by providing home-like chairs and settees for feeding and socialising, as well as children's chairs and tables suited to their age and size, easily moved, rearranged and carried by older toddlers. Furniture for home play, book corners and quiet areas for very young children does not need to be complex, but carefully selected for size, comfort, realism and flexibility as well as just for durability.

Key features of an effective environment for babies and toddlers

The furnishings and equipment should contribute to the sense of calm discussed earlier in this chapter. Although colour is important, the almost violent primary colours of many children's toys are not what we would choose for the walls and furniture of our own homes, and we would be wise to adopt the calming pastels and natural colours of most homes, enlivening these with splashes or points of colour, which are easily changed. Natural objects, an aquarium, some growing plants or flowers, and even some ornaments can also make your environment more homely and welcoming for children and their families.

Some research into the effect of different colours on behaviour and mood could also be useful – choosing calming greens and blues in areas where babies and children rest and sleep, and reserving red and dark blue for areas where we want the children to feel hungry or active. Remember, deep red, blue and green are the signature colours of action – that is why superheroes are always portrayed in such colours, and children will respond to them too. So if you want action, paint your walls red and blue, but don't then complain about the noise!

In most homes, music and voices are constant companions, with radio, TV and other sounds filling our days, and this can make a setting seem very strange – for some it may seem overly quiet, for others overly noisy! Be aware of the sounds of your setting. I would not recommend that you have music radio on all day, although many parents do, but there is a place for music, and for sounds made by wind chimes, CDs of natural sounds such as birdsong or water, or an open window for sounds of the world outside.

The sense of smell is very powerful and one we sometimes overlook when reviewing the homeliness of our settings. Most of us can remember the smell of our first school, and for me it was a combination of sour milk, dust, strong disinfectant and children's hot bodies. This smell was hard-wired by frequent experience as I attended the school each day, and a simple whiff of that combination brings back feelings of dread for me! But in these days, clean does not need to smell antiseptic, fresh air can combat most odours, and the judicious use of a subtle room spray can make all the difference for a shared setting in a community centre redolent of last night's judo class.

Some of the schools in Reggio Emilia in Italy actually pipe the cooking smells from their kitchens into their settings, so the children can smell and look forward to lunchtime together, and even look through specially placed windows to watch the cook at work.

So a 'home away from home' needs too appeal to all our senses, and really resemble the homes of the children who attend, making the transition from home to care as easy and comfortable as possible.

Space

Space is also a vital ingredient in effective settings. Cramped, over-furnished, cluttered places, or cold, hard and cavernous spaces will work against the essential home-from-home. Our own homes combine spaces to be warm and cosy, spaces to do energetic or messy things, spaces to eat and sleep, and young children need these too. Floors with warm surfaces, where babies can lie, and later roll, crawl, creep and toddle, both indoors and outside, are essential for babies and toddlers.

Of course, these spaces should be carefully supervised to ensure safety and a sense of security, particularly when babies are on the floor, and how you protect floor-based babies from the rampaging of older, more mobile children, can be a constant tension, but one which should not be ignored by restricting either group. Babies, both lying and sitting, need a safe place where they can be on the floor, and this can be provided by simple measures such as moving low level furniture to create a barrier, making a simple change in floor surface or colour, or looking at your setting to locate a corner where babies can still see what is going on without being on one of the movement routes of older children.

Other spaces will include places to be active and enthusiastic, places to explore and create, and comfortable places to sit with friends to share a story or a chat. Some settings use a system of organisation based on areas of interest or curriculum activities such as a block area, a book area, a creative area and a role-play area, separated by low furniture or screens. In baby and toddler rooms, the children will use resources anywhere in the room, and outside, constantly on the move, and not very interested in the careful organisation of the practitioners. A more successful model for these young children may be to provide lots of low shelving with baskets of toys and other resources stored logically in groups, where children can see and select what they need, taking it to their chosen play space. This organisation will leave plenty of space in the middle of the room for the sort of flowing play that children of this age enjoy.

Flexibility is also important; think again about our homes and how we use them. We use spaces flexibly, sleeping on the settee, eating in the garden, ironing where we can see the TV, reading in the bathroom, free to choose quiet or company as our mood suggests. Children need to be able to use the spaces flexibly too, making a picnic in the middle of the floor, constructing a train or bus with chairs, using the space under a bush as a den, and they usually like to be able to see other people, even if they are in a tunnel or under a table.

As you work in your setting, watch the children and see where they choose to play. Do they like corners and hidey-holes? Do they play under furniture? Do they take lots of things outside to play with? Do they like big spaces or do these make them cluster round the edges or race around madly in the middle? As you observe the children, think creatively about how you could reorganise your room or the whole of your setting to reflect the needs of the current group.

Some settings have removed cots from their baby rooms, preferring to have mattresses and cushioned areas, or even individual soft pet beds for babies to rest on, thus creating more space for play and exploration, as well as giving babies a sense of control over when and where they sleep. Other practitioners have removed some of the more formal tables and chairs, replacing these with children's armchairs, garden sets, cushions and carpet pieces, so babies and toddlers can feel at home and comfortable, and can move these into different combinations.

Places to be with other babies, children and adults

Babies love and thrive on company, and simple activities such as peeping through the cot sides at another baby, riding in a double buggy, dancing with another baby in the arms of a carer, or sharing a rug on the floor can be rewarding encounters. Babies also love being with and watching older children, so we should try to provide 'family groupings' for at least part of the day, where babies and older children can share the same spaces, as they naturally do in families. As they grow and become toddlers, children often choose to play alongside their peers, before they embark on collaborative or cooperative play. Practitioners should recognise that opportunities for social play are key contributions to development made by early years settings.

Pop-up tents (indoors and in the garden), floor cushions, carpet squares and bean bags all provide comfortable places to be, and if you have space, you might add small mattresses, settee cushions or small settees, window seats or cushion cubes. Your garden also needs places for talking and watching – garden benches, picnic tables, swing chairs and hammocks, children's garden chairs, even climbing plants and living willow can provide pleasant places to sit in the sun or the shade.

When considering these sorts of places for talk and shared play, it is useful to take into account the needs of adults as well as children. No child wants to have an adult looming over them while they are involved in play, and adults need to be able to get down to children's level. Younger practitioners may find it easy to get down to floor level to join play (and get up again after!) but we all need somewhere to 'perch' – a low chair, garden bench or other half-way place so eye contact can be maintained and intrusion kept to a minimum.

Free choice

This is a vital component in successful environments, and brain research indicates that most babies and children will use free choice to practise and revisit their current interests, often in schematic play. This repetitive play is essential for turning soft-wiring between brain cells into hard-wired skills by laying down a protective coating of myelin over the connections. It is now evident that one of the reasons why children 'fret or flit' when they are offered free choice is not because they can't choose, but because they can't see or get what they need for the next stage in their learning. Cupboard doors, high shelves, closed boxes and cluttered storage are often at fault, and a simple reorganisation of the room will usually enable children to find and concentrate on the things that interest them.

Try to understand the frustration of having a few toys chosen for you and put on the available tables, or being presented with a toy chosen by an adult, when you can clearly see what you really want, but don't know how to

say it. This would drive even the most patient of us to distraction! It is no wonder that children 'fret or flit' without settling or concentrating if they are making do with playthings that we have selected.

In the best settings, choice is provided for even the youngest babies, with adults watching for interests, and responding to body language and other ways of requesting or showing interest. Adults take babies to the objects and toys, respond to choices made through eye-pointing and gesture, make access easy for crawlers and bottom shufflers, and encourage toddlers to select, collect and help to return the toys and equipment they have chosen to play with.

Getting the storage right is also essential, and removing cupboard doors, using low shelves where children can see what they want, putting equipment in several small baskets rather than one big one, using clear plastic boxes where the contents are visible, and labelling containers with a photo or piece of equipment will all help children to see what they need and, more importantly, to get it for themselves. Of course, for many two year olds, the thing they may want to practise is whether the shelves would be better with nothing on them and everything on the floor (a trajectory schema), or if the Lego and the Sticklebricks would look good mixed up in a handbag (a filling and emptying schema)!

Respect

Respect for children's views, personal growth and individuality, their families, cultures, backgrounds and needs is a big factor in provision. In excellent settings, every child is respected as an individual, not only in encouraging choices but in recognising the uniqueness of each child.

Respect is apparent in the way photos of families are displayed on walls and in books, personal comfort objects are carefully stored where adults and children can find them in time of need and cultural elements of children's lives are included in role-play areas, books, signs and posters. Even before children can distinguish words in different languages, they will recognise the familiar objects from their own lives, and the messages to parents will affect the way they relate to the setting too.

Right from the beginning of their time in a setting, before the child can use it independently, a personal place or space is important. Boxes, drawers, locker units, coat pegs, shoe bags, each labelled with a picture or name, are all examples of the respect paid by the practitioners to the personal belongings of individual children, and as they move from babyhood, children will take real ownership of the special place for a toy from home, their new hat and gloves or other reminders of home.

Respect is shown, not only in the way children are treated but in the way practitioners model respect for the environment and the equipment it contains. Of course, the setting will get disorganised during a session, particularly when children are choosing and discarding playthings. However, in a place of respect, order is restored regularly during the day, toys and equipment are stored in predictable places, and the condition of resources is well-maintained. This does not mean being obsessive about tidiness or restricting children's freedom to access their chosen resources, it is about pride in place, beauty in the environment and shared responsibility.

Places with a sense of proper order are well organised: the storage and equipment is well labelled and attractively arranged in quantities suited to the ages of the children; objects of interest, plants and flowers are carefully included; broken or damaged equipment is promptly repaired or removed; shared areas such as the entrance are tidy and attractive; washrooms, changing areas and kitchens are clean and pleasant to use. This sense of order is not lost on parents or their children!

Another aspect of the respectful setting is the way in which practitioners select resources and objects to reflect a truly inclusive view of childhood, the local community and the wider world. There are many ways to achieve this, and not just by eating noodles on Chinese New Year. Inclusive thinking permeates high quality settings, from the staffing policy to the books in book corners; from the words and pictures displayed to the range of visitors invited to meet the children. Inclusive respect isn't just about wheelchair access or a multicultural poster, it runs through the whole setting like the name in a stick of rock.

Free access to a garden

Babies and young children love being out of doors, and should be able to be in a garden whenever they feel the need. Such free access, commonly referred to as 'free flow' is an ideal, which many settings try to achieve, and they realise the benefits of free access to the garden as a right, not a gift bestowed by the adults at a special time or in good weather. It is not always possible to provide free flow play, but the way in which the outside and inside of the setting relate and are used is a key indicator of high quality provision.

Even in settings where babies and older children use different areas of the garden, access should be easy and frequent. In high quality settings babies use the garden as much as older children, and some make provision for resting or sleeping out of doors. In other settings, the doors to the garden are permanently open, and once babies are on the move, they can indicate their wish to be outside by using ramps or wide, shallow steps provided just for them. Careful and sensitive supervision by staff ensures that babies do not embark on these adventures alone!

Older babies and toddlers access the garden freely in all weathers, and learn early how to find and put on waterproof clothing and boots. They know that resources are available and accessible outside, and that additional things from indoors can be added to those already provided in the garden. In addition to the usual wheeled toys and climbing apparatus, these resources include plenty of 'loose parts' – small and larger items that can be assembled and re-assembled in different ways, for different purposes. Natural objects such as stones, cones, leaves and sticks are there, as are materials such as boxes and fabrics for making dens and shelters; places to watch weather, insects and birds; places to be quiet and relax; places to dig and grow things. In this toddler version of the pre-school garden, flexible resources are of a smaller scale, but none the less exciting and challenging.

As in the inside spaces, the garden is not always tidy, but there is a sense of order alongside the sense of excitement and innovation as practitioners provide resources to interest individuals and groups. There are opportunities to share in simple activities such as planting bulbs and vegetables, filling bird feeders, watching minibeasts, erecting pop-up tents, using water to pour, spray and paint, or stamping in puddles. These are initiated by practitioners who have observed the emerging interests of individuals and small groups, or from a desire to use the garden to stimulate every muscle and every sense.

And the garden extends into the community, with small walks to the park, the shops, the Post Office or the garden centre, providing the stimulus for further play as children revisit the experiences in role play. This garden is a true 'kindergarten' – a garden for, and a garden of children, where babies and toddlers can be free to explore the natural world in safety and with the support of caring adults.

Supportive and professional adults

As we have already emphasised, these are one of the most important resources available to the children. They ensure that every child feels attached and in tune with their lives, both in the setting and through the careful transitions to and from home. These adults do not attempt to replace parents. They realise that being a key person is a responsibility with significant differences from parenthood, and they take this responsibility seriously. They carefully manage the multiple demands of group care, curriculum organisation, and a focus on individual children, but always put a premium of time and attention on the best interests of individuals, never forgetting that the children belong to their family first.

> *'The key person approach is a way of working in settings in which the whole focus and organisation is aimed at enabling and supporting close attachments between individual children and individual staff. The Key Person approach is an involvement, an individual and reciprocal commitment between a member of staff and a family.'*
> *Wellbeing from Birth*, Rosemary Roberts (Sage, 2010).

Resources to support brain development

At the heart of provision for babies and very young children are their warm and loving relationships with other people, adults and other children. These relationships are essential, but this is not all! Babies and young children (the crawlers, creepers, standers and wobbling walkers) need a stimulating and inspiring environment, full of objects that excite them, sparking brain cells into action and encouraging them to communicate with each other.

> *'Positive experiences, such as exposure to rich learning opportunities, and negative influences, such as malnutrition or environmental toxins, leave a chemical "signature" on the genes, which can be temporary or permanent.'*
> 'The Timing and Quality of Early Years Experiences Combine to Shape Brain Architecture': Working Paper 5 (National Scientific Council on the Developing Child, Harvard University, 2008).

How some familiar resources support brain building.

There are many resources that continue to be essential in provision when thinking about a rich and stimulating environment for babies and young children, and the reasons for their continuing popularity with children emerges as research into early brain building continues. Posting boxes, buckets, and connecting blocks support the development of schematic play, a key component of myelination and hard-wiring of learning. Hats, bags, dolls and soft toys, tea sets, cloaks, crowns and shoes are essentials of role-play, pretending and imagining other roles and other worlds where there are problems to be solved and stories to be played out. Small worlds help children to play out their lives in miniature, revisiting experiences and playing many parts. Books, songs, puppets, soft toys and simple music support communication and a growing sense of empathy. Climbing frames, wheeled toys, barrows and tools, as well as sand, water and dough play help to build muscles and movement.

These clues from research help us to provide the best range of resources for learning, for wiring and for practising what emerges from rich experiences, so the learning becomes permanent and protected. But any equipment list can be used as a guide or as a painful stick to make you feel inadequate. For babies and toddlers, the key criteria when setting up or evaluating your setting must follow the essentials set out above, answering the single question: How can we make a home from home where parents and their children come first and practitioners know that their place is with the children?

Moving on up – what do children need from three to six?

Although the years from pre-birth to three are crucial times in brain and body development, it is now clear that rapid brain development continues far beyond these years, and that the first phase of major development lasts at least until the child is six or seven. Both hard and soft-wiring continue, at different rates in different children. Some will spend major parts of the years from three to six in myelinating (practising) the softer connections, repeating favourite or familiar activities until they are part of the permanent architecture of the brain. These children will return again and again to the train set or the building blocks as they reinforce their knowledge about movement, stability, connection and construction.

Others will continue to spend more time enriching their soft-wiring map, thirsting for new experiences and activities and different paths for learning. They will engage enthusiastically with every new opportunity or experience, seemingly getting a real 'buzz' from the novelty, and sometimes having a visible 'Eureka' moment as they join new connections to more established ones.

Yet other young learners will spend at least some periods of time reaffirming their hard-wired knowledge, including some of the features wired at birth (such as thumb sucking), and appearing to make little 'progress', and even regressing as they adjust to their changing environment. These children watch a lot, play in parallel, test boundaries and still need a lot of support as they confirm that what they already know and can do is still useful and true. They may also show signs of behaviour that they had apparently grown out of, such as clinging, weeping or tantrums.

All these behaviours are quite normal! They are also the reasons why the environment should not change dramatically as children reach three years old, or four, five or six, because continuing to offer familiar toys, activities, people and other resources as well as new experiences will meet

Reinforcing soft wiring and turning it into hard wiring.

the needs of all the children, as they move forward on their individual learning pathways, using the resources in old and new ways.

> *Children in this older age group are still likely to swing back and forth in development, depending on their moods and the context, but they have a growing capacity for coping with unpredictability and change, especially if they are anchored by emotional support, respect, and acceptance.*
>
> *Te Whariki Early Childhood Curriculum*
> (Ministry of Education, New Zealand, 1996).

Growing independence

All children from three to six still need the essentials of both attachment and attunement, and this can cause tensions as they also become increasingly interested in independence. Just like children under three, they still need to feel *attached* to the people who care for them – their parents and their principal carers in day care or school, but they want to be free of these constraints for some of the time, returning regularly for assurance that the adults are still there. In this period, the ratios for key person groups also change, until at the age of five or six, the teacher takes over the key person responsibility for the whole group, which can be anywhere between 12 and 30 children.

Of course, by this time, the routines of bodily care, such as toileting, getting drinks and feeding are usually managed independently by the children themselves. Many of the routines of the setting, such as preparing activities, clearing up and putting away toys and equipment become

The continuing need for both attainment and attunement.

responsibilities shared with the adults, although children will sometimes find ways of avoiding or delaying their share of this responsibility!

Children's growing independence moves the attachment relationship into a different phase, where the child is still free to organise their own learning for some of the time, selecting where, who and what to play with, but the demands of the early years curriculum begin to intervene. The adult begins to readjust their role, from being responsive play partner to focusing more on the roles of teacher and mentor. Most children cope easily with these changes from room to room, place to place, year to year, often anticipating the new situation with enthusiasm. However, for a minority, the gradual distancing of adult relationships, compounded by the change in adult/child ratios, can sometimes catapult children into forced independence before they are emotionally or socially ready, and these are the children who appear to revert to hard-wired responses, including crying, hitting, grabbing or flitting from activity to activity.

Boys, who are more susceptible to separation anxiety, and may develop social and emotional competence at a later age, are more likely to feel abandoned, but without the maturity to realise why, and the consequences of this can be unacceptable behaviour brought on by insecurity. Boys, in fact, tend to be far more securely attached to their key person than girls, who develop emotional competence earlier, enabling them to cope with the dilution of attachment by relying more heavily on their friends – and many girls make life-long relationships at this stage of their development.

> Some children develop more slowly and will need elements of the environment from earlier stages.

This change for children, and the adults who care for them, means a shift in the notion of responsive care for the practitioner too. In excellent settings and schools the practitioner steps back a little from participating in all the action, but continues to watch and respond with sensitivity to the needs of individuals and small groups within the class. This practitioner/ teacher/mentor is no longer solely the valued play partner, she is the observer, noting current interests and emerging skills, and scaffolding children's learning by providing a continuing rich environment where the next steps in learning can take place. In Maria Montessori's words:

> 'The teacher's first duty is to watch over the environment, and this takes precedence over all the rest. Its influence is indirect, but unless it be well done there will be no effective and permanent results of any kind, physical, intellectual or spiritual.'
>
> Dr Montessori's own Handbook, Maria Montessori
> (Schocken Books 1965).

Metacognition

But this is not enough! Just watching and providing will not necessarily lead to secure learning. At the stage between three and six, children need to express their thinking in words, clarifying concepts by discussing, asking questions, problem solving and evaluating, and adults and other children are key players in this activity. Scientists call this process metacognition, thinking about thinking, and it is evident that, although babies and toddlers do a lot of thinking, exploring, and even problem solving, three year olds are the ones who begin to get this process out and talk about it. The process of metacognition, and its development through conversations and provocations is also referred to as 'sustained shared thinking'. It is one of the key indicators of effective settings, identified by the Effective Provision of Pre-school Education (EPPE) research carried out in England, which offers the following description of the adult role in effective settings:

The emerging importance of thinking skills.

> 'Effective pedagogy includes interaction traditionally associated with the term 'teaching', the provision of instructive learning environments and 'sustained shared thinking' to extend children's learning.'
> National School Improvement Network 'Research Matters' No 21,
> The Effective Provision of Pre-school Education (EPPE) Project
> (Institute of Education, University of London, 2003).

Three-part role of the practitioner

This research has brought the three-part role of the early years practitioner – teaching, providing a stimulating environment, and helping children to think by thinking with them – to the centre of policy and practice in early years settings in England and many other countries.

Sustained shared thinking is described as a situation where:

> ... two or more individuals work together in a cognitive way to solve a problem, clarify a concept, evaluate an activity, extend a narrative etc. Both parties must contribute to the thinking and it must develop and extend the understanding.
> National School Improvement Network 'Research Matters' No 21,
> The Effective Provision of Pre-school Education (EPPE) Project
> (Institute of Education, University of London, 2003).

So the adult's role makes a subtle shift during a substantial portion of the day from being a *play* partner into being a declared *thinking* partner, sharing the learning with the child. Nevertheless, we also have clear guidance that the adult must still stay attached, because children need secure attachment if they are to develop the essential skills of thinking and talking about thinking.

Role-play

The brains of young children, still very plastic, continue to make thousands of connections every second, constructing an individual map of their learning about the world, and revisiting concepts to adjust and refine the details of fine motor control, understanding and confidence.

The continuing importance of role play.

Children from three to six spend a huge amount of time being someone else, and this is an essential feature of the environment for three to six year olds.

The first simple role-play of brushing hair or feeding teddy has now developed into an ability to adopt an alternative persona for long periods of time, weaving behaviours and experiences into complex characters. The superhero puts the baby to bed before flying off to rescue someone; children in the home corner become so obsessed with the details of the family they are creating that an additional child is forced to become the dog, so it does not interrupt the flow of relationships; a small boy spends all day in a princess dress, refusing to answer to any name but Your Royal Highness; another refuses to come to the table for a meal unless a place is also laid for her imaginary friend Beatrix, and two children earnestly explore the consequences of the death of a character in a story. We all know these children and marvel at their creativity, but recent research into the way children think now reveals that they are doing more than just playing roles.

Alison Gopnik has collated much of the research into how children think, and has come up with some very interesting insights, particularly into the place of role-play in child development. Her book, *The Philosophical Baby* (Bodley Head, 2009) (which in fact talks in depth about not just babies, but children from birth to six) proposes that all play, including role-play and imaginary friendships, helps children to explore all the possible ways their knowledge of the world could be combined and applied. This is a combination of hypothesis and fiction – not far from the late-night discussions adolescents have about the existence of parallel universes, or when we imagine what we would do if we won the Lottery; or when a child hypothesises about what they would do if they were a superhero and had a baby.

It is a visible way of exploring soft-wiring – lots of journeys down partial knowledge, revisiting different aspects of the world and combining them in new ways, and in so doing reaffirming and expanding knowledge. It is very evident that children know that when they are exploring in this way their play is not real, just as we know we couldn't win the Lottery because we never even buy a ticket – this does not stop us from thinking about it, and children think aloud in their play, using their bodies as well as their minds and voices as tools for thinking as they go about their imagined worlds.

The role of counterfactual thinking in helping children make sense of their experiences.

Counterfactual thinking

The philosophical definition of these make-believe worlds and role-play games is 'counterfactuals', things Alison Gopnik describes as 'the woulda-coulda-shouldas of life, all the things that might happen in the future, but haven't yet, or that could have happened in the past but didn't quite'. She says that in role-play, children are using elements of their knowledge to prepare all sorts of alternative blueprints for behaviour, which has the capability of changing the past, the present or, in particular, the future, and these counterfactual creations are called stories. She maintains that although being a prolific role-player in pre-school does not predict a career in journalism or writing the next Harry Potter series, it is very close to the activity of writing fiction, which takes these counterfactuals of our lives out of our adult brains and onto the page or the screen!

> 'The three-year-old pretending to be a fairy princess isn't just being adorable and creative, she's also demonstrating a uniquely human kind of intelligence.'
> *The Philosophical Baby*, Alison Gopnik (Bodley Head, 2009).

Role-play is therefore a very creative way for children to practise what they know about the world by rearranging it in ways that enable them to understand the past, manage the present and influence the future. This should make us even more determined to provide the time, space and flexible resources that make role-play rich and varied, and we should be including whole-body role-play with props and clothes, hats, bags, shoes, crowns, helmets, masks and cloaks. This should be supported by small world play of all sorts, where miniature figures can become children's alter-egos, playing out their counterfactual stories by proxy.

Blocks, bricks, den-building materials and all sorts of other flexible-use materials such as wheels, boxes, buckets, baskets and boxes, drainpipes and guttering will encourage free creative play. Items (sometimes called 'loose parts', see page 46) which can be transformed into many things are also essential for creative story play – stones, sticks, small blocks, counters, coins, fabrics, string, cones, shells, big seeds, small bottles and jars – representing money, magic tokens, food, treasure or potions in the counterfactual thinking. Add some writing implements and paper, and you have an even richer recipe for complex thinking through play.

If we watch children who are not in daytime care or school, most of their day is spent in counterfactual activity. They play out the stories they see on TV and DVD; they imitate older siblings and their parents in complex family dramas, using dolls and soft toys as characters; they invent imaginary friends who only eat special food or live in special beds and they make up counterfactual events to cover their mistakes or misdemeanours, such as 'A big boy came and ate the cookies', in an attempt to change something that has already happened by creating a new version of reality. As children get older, they practise being other children with more adventurous or extreme behaviours, by adopting these in front of a mirror or even with their parents.

Play is an essential of life and we don't stop needing it when we leave the nursery. Even children who are well adjusted and come from stable backgrounds need to explore the world of counterfactuals, and we should ensure that they have the opportunities in our schools and settings to do so. Sustained shared thinking is very useful way to explore the counterfactual worlds of children, as we ponder with them on the 'whys?' 'what ifs?' 'wheres?' and 'hows' of metacognition or 'thinking about thinking'.

Children learn better when they are in tune with the environment.

Brain development

Children will get the most out of play situations when they feel both attached and in tune with the environment and the people who inhabit it with them. Well-attached children, those who feel secure and confident will learn more and retain more of what they learn. In Chapter 3 there is an explanation of the process of myelination, the laying down of a fatty covering that protects and improves links between brain cells. This process continues through most of our lives, but the time between birth and about ten years old is the prime time for building the complex architecture of the brain, and laying down much of the hard-wiring needed for lifelong learning.

As workers in the early years, we need to know how myelin works and what endangers its formation, so we can protect this amazing process and prevent it from damage. Myelin is a substance that insulates and protects the links between brain cells, and helps them to transmit messages more quickly. However, there is a down side to myelin – it is very susceptible to stress, carried to the brain as stress hormones such as cortisol, produced by our bodies when we feel misunderstood, frustrated, angry or scared. These stress hormones actually erode myelin sheathing from brain connections, exposing the neural connections beneath to chemicals and undermining their ability to communicate. When this happens, we feel even more frustrated, and children, particularly boys, will often display violent and unacceptable behaviour.

Some children are unfortunate in having stressful experiences at home, and may enter our settings and schools every day suffering the effects of cortisol, which can be compounded if they are again frustrated in play, or by their inability to conform to the demands of the setting. Boys, because they may be six months behind in their readiness for a more concentrated curriculum, will find it difficult to control their frustration, and may explode in intense physical activity, tantrums or aggression.

The role of stress in reducing children's capacity to learn.

However, this does not mean we should try to eliminate stress entirely from our schools and settings. There is 'chronic stress' – the stress that arises from living in a family where violence or extreme poverty prevail, which damages memory and can even reduce the size of some parts of the brain – and there is what Jane Healey calls 'good stress' which enhances learning:

> 'Challenge without excess threat is the secret – the positive feeling of tackling a manageable difficulty with the promise of success. This kind of learning energises the cortex and helps establish memory. Trying to make learning too much easy 'fun' robs it of both challenge and joy.'
> Your Child's Growing Mind, Jane M. Healey (Broadway, 2004).

If we combine what Jane Healey is saying with the thoughts of Alison Gopnik, and the findings of the EPPE research, we can clearly see a recipe for successful early learning. This requires a stress-free environment, plenty of time for counterfactual play, the presence of others with whom children can scaffold and extend their thinking in talk, and adults who spend time with children and respond to the needs they observe – continuation of early responsive care or attunement. This is eloquently described in the curriculum for early childhood in New Zealand:

> *Young children (from 3–6) need:*
> - *adults and environments to provide resources, challenges, and support for their widening interests and problem-solving capacities;*
> - *opportunities for unfamiliar routines, new and self-directed challenges, co-operative ventures, and sustained projects;*
> - *adults who can encourage sustained conversations, queries, and complex thinking, including concepts of fairness, difference, and similarity;*
> - *opportunities to use language to explore and to direct thinking and learning tasks;*
> - *a widening range of resources for creative expression, symbolising, and representation;*
> - *recognition of their developing sense of humour, which springs from new understandings about how things "ought" to be;*
> - *challenging opportunities which keep pace with their physical co-ordination and development.*
>
> *Te Whariki Early Childhood Curriculum*
> (Ministry of Education, New Zealand, 1996).

Essential requirements for three to six year olds

Drawing together these key indicators of a successful approach for three to six years olds will result in a quartet of essentials similar, but with significant complexities, to those required for under threes:

Attachment

Children continue to need secure attachment, a feeling that they are important and well known in their school or setting. The key person is still vital in the equation, and key people for three year olds are still very much attached to and informed about the family, with frequent contact and small numbers in their key groups. However, as children reach school age, the key person may well be supporting every child in the group or class, and so may not have time for the daily contact given at earlier stages. If transfer of

Children continue to need to feel attached and in tune, and still need key people to support them.

information between setting and school is good, and parents are committed to keeping channels of communication open, children can still expect to be well known and to have some individualised provision. The Early Years Foundation Stage guidance in England gives this description of key person roles in school:

> 'Even when children are older and can hold key people from home in mind for longer, there is still a need for them to have a key person to depend on in the setting, such as their teacher or teaching assistant.'
> *Practice Guidance for the Early Years Foundation Stage*
> (Department for Education and Skills, 2007).

Responsive care, or attunement

As children grow older, their need for people who are genuinely interested in them does not diminish, in their unique needs and their unique families. In fact, children need to expand their personal circle of people, both adults and children, who are important to them. Most three year olds are able to relate to all the adults in the room, and by the time children are five, it is assumed that most children no longer need such intense care from a named key person. They do still need an individualised approach within their class and, of course, children with additional needs should continue to benefit from a key person who knows their circumstances in detail. By the time children are six, many are confident enough to relate to children who are much older, and to adults in the school and the community who are less familiar.

> 'When children and adults work together in an active learning setting with supportive social climate, children are motivated to carry out their own intentions. Adults encourage children to use what they know to solve problems and initiate new experiences from which they gain new insights. In this open-ended approach, learn through experience and construct their own understanding of the world.'
> *Educating Young Children*, Mary Hohmann and David P. Weikart
> (High/Scope Press, 2002).

Predictability and routine; a sense of calm

These are essentials in any learning environment. Children need to know where to find, and increasingly where to return, the resources they need and use. They need to understand that the setting or school is a place of order, with necessary rules and expectations for children and adults, as in the High/Scope 'supportive social climate'. As children get older, there should also be an underlying buzz of excitement and

The need for a flexible timetable which balances the need for security with providing child-friendly time.

anticipation as they plan their own activities, select and organise resources, and increasingly manage their own learning.

The predictable timetable for the day gives security, but it is not a straightjacket, restricting children's initiative or cramping their concentration. The planning of the daily schedule should have a loose but predictable framework, and everyone should be able to accept a degree of flexibility.

'Children who become involved in a learning activity should be given the opportunity to continue with it for as long as they need. Teachers need to find ways of making space for work in progress rather than simply telling children to clear up at the end of the day'.
The Reggio Emilia Approach to Early Years Education, Marianne Valentine (Scottish Consultative Council on the Curriculum, 1999).

'Children's settings require ordered time and space – space that furthers the program's goals while making the program a pleasant place to lie and work for all those who inhabit the program. What it needs is planned complexity – and environment rich enough to challenge, but not so complex as to frustrate.'
Caring Spaces, Learning Places, Jim Greenman (Exchange Press, 1988).

It is now clear from research that children take at least ten seconds to respond to a question posed by an adult, and they rarely get this thinking time. We do still need to slow down to what Jim Greenman describes as 'children's time', and sadly the effect of that is often to place stress on an already pressured adult schedule.

We need to get our priorities straight – children between three and six need a good balance of activity and calm, of adult intervention and child initiation, of small group and smaller group. Yet adults are constantly being pressured into moving at a fast and furious pace, with learning goals rather than children's needs driving them. Cracking that conundrum will take persistence, even stubbornness on the part of the adults, who are the ones who have the power to do the right thing with the children in their care!

Adults as an essential element of the environment

In Wales, unlike many other countries including England, the early years curriculum spans the age range from three to seven years. In other countries, pre-school provision and school are much more separate, so I am quoting here from the Welsh guidance document for the Foundation Stage:

> 'Practitioners need to plan the learning environment very carefully to ensure that the children are having a range of play/active learning activities that allow them to be spontaneous, as well as participating in structured directed activities. The learning environment should be inviting, stimulating, flexible, language rich and used as a powerful resource to motivate learners.'
>
> *Play/Active Learning: Overview for 3 to 7-year-olds*
> (Department for Children, Education and Lifelong Learning and Skills, Welsh Assembly Government, 2008).

The learning environment for three to six year olds should be just as rich and stimulating as that for babies and younger children.

We don't only need the best teacher/practitioners in the baby, toddler and pre-school rooms of early education, we need them right through the primary years as well, and recent amalgamation of infant and nursery provision into all-through primary schools has sometimes made it difficult to protect the specific needs of the youngest. The advantages of all-through primary schools, include smoother progression and the inevitable financial advantages of size, but, unless the senior managers appointed to the key posts in these wide age-range schools are vigilant, then the unique nature of early years education will be lost.

If a whole primary school adopts an approach based on the evidence of brain research and the principles of active, cross-curricular learning, thinking skills and social awareness from nursery age (and some do), then there is little problem with understanding what is going on in the groups where under sevens are learning.

The importance of having practitioners/ teachers who are knowledgeable about the unique nature of early learning.

However, in some primary/elementary schools, and even in the few remaining 'infant' schools or kindergartens, the management team can get skewed towards focusing on the needs of the older children rather than the youngest. Combine this with a recent and growing emphasis on targets and league tables (as in parts of the UK and in the USA), and we have a situation where *what* children learn is becoming more important than *how* they learn.

Continuing to provide a 'rich and stimulating environment' through these years is a challenge, even for teacher/practitioners with long experience of working with the age range. Younger professionals, who may have had less time to get to grips with the needs of three to six year olds could fall into the trap of thinking 'What these younger children need is a simpler version of what older children get'. However, when all the research into how to mend our 'broken society' is telling us that early intervention is crucial, that we should make early years settings more like homes, and primary schools more like the most excellent early years settings, it seems astonishing that many of those who advise and inspect teachers, as well as the governments that pay for much of the research, are apparently happy to ignore their findings and recommendations.

Adults in high quality, responsive and supportive environments for thinking will need to know how to find out children's current stage of learning, so they need a good grounding in child development, including some of the latest research findings which have overturned some of the long respected opinions of Piaget and Freud. They also need to be good watchers, listeners, and co-learners, because the standard, often subject-based primary curriculum won't do for these children. They need something much more integrated, much less rigid, which flourishes on new ideas and individual interests, acknowledging each new group as unique with unique needs. It should be built on observing the children *first*, then planning to meet needs and emerging abilities and interests, not just planning in a vacuum and then delivering activities that are assessed at the end.

Key features of environments for three to six year olds

Key features of high quality environments for three to six year olds need to include many of the essentials for earlier years, and if you look at Chapter 6, you will find that the equipment lists suggest that each stage needs all or most of the equipment for the stage before, but with options to use it in different ways to meet the demands of growing minds. Three to six year olds need:

A continuing home away from home.

This will be essential to support role-play – counterfactual explorations of what it is like to be someone else, to behave in different ways, and to explore experiences. However, this home-based play, although it allows Superman to come to our house, is not always enough as children begin to widen their knowledge of places, people and things.

Being out and about in their community will result in the need to be the fireman, the nurse, the vet, the shopkeeper or the builder. Books, stories, TV and DVD will spark imaginative roles, as characters and events from imagined places are played out. Of course, children will still be exploring ways of combining these, the pirate will wheel his treasure around in the wheelbarrow, the bridesmaid will take the baby shopping, and the vet will energetically use his stethoscope to examine people as well as soft toys. Furniture in rooms for three to six year olds should still be child-scale, flexible in use and easily moved by the children, so they can increasingly be involved in creating their own places for learning.

Other areas where settings and schools can provide homely places and homely items will include libraries, quiet areas and story corners, where sofas, cushions and domestic lighting can create a softer atmosphere and in the garden, where seats, swings, planters and flowers can make a more home-like place. Entrance ways, porches and communal areas can also be made more welcoming to children and their families by adding living plants, fabrics, cushions and domestic furniture.

Maintaining a calm atmosphere should always be a priority, as children need calm and quiet places throughout the setting. Because children will gradually be expected to stay longer at activities as their concentration span lengthens, it is important to watch and monitor how and where children choose to play. Some children like to play lying down on the carpet; some make for particular corners of the room or the garden when they wish to be left undisturbed; some need a less active place to read and play with small apparatus in the garden.

Consider how you could help the 'always in the garden' children to find a place indoors when the weather is inclement; how you could tempt the 'never in the creative area' to get involved with paint and clay; or how you could encourage writing in the garden for children who find writing indoors a chore and a stress. These reflections, and your observations, will help you to protect the places children like, and perhaps to make more of these sorts of spaces, and less of the neutral, stressful and often less used table and chair space. Here are two descriptions of early years rooms:

'The classroom was spotless as the three year old children entered. Gleaming tile floors, walls and tables; a tidy carpeted area; orderly, well stocked shelves; cheerful teachers; cheery murals and bulletin boards …. All day long the children were busy at tables, in the block corner, in the housekeeping area, or in activities with the teachers. The routines were efficient – lunch and snack were downed, the children slept, nose were wiped, more activities were performed, and the children went home. But something was missing, something important. When the children were gone again, there was no imprint, none of the general residue or artefacts of lived lives. The care and education were there, but it was a place devoid of feeling, of character, of real warmth.'

Caring Spaces, Learning Places Jim Greenman
(Exchange Press, 1988).

In this room, the adults are clearly in control of the activities and of the environment. No-one could fault their commitment or their hard work in keeping their setting clean and the children safe and well occupied, but every evening, all traces of the children are either put away, swept away, or carefully mounted to be added to displays, leaving a clean canvas for a new day. Real learning is not like that, as we know from our own homes where 'work in progress' litters our lives – not just the ironing basket and the washing up, but the magazine we are reading, the card we need to write, the shopping list or the bills waiting to be paid, the packet of free seeds waiting to be planted – children's bedrooms, in particular, are full of these works in progress.

Compare this environment with the classroom of some five and six year olds, recently visited after the children had gone home:

This room is also clean and has a shiny floor, but this is not the first thing you notice. Everywhere in this colourful environment there is evidence of learning initiated by the children themselves, and valued by the adults who work with them. In several places in the room, there are unfinished creations – home-made books are carefully placed in the writing area, ready to be continued tomorrow, half completed Lego models labelled 'Sam, please do not touch' sit on a shelf; the table in the tiny home corner has been carefully laid by a child, ready for tomorrow's

play; a home-made forest provides an environment for some fairy figures, and a large puppet sits on an adult chair, holding a favourite storybook. On a whiteboard is a reminder, in a child's writing, to go out tomorrow and look for signs of the bulbs the children planted in the school grounds last autumn.

The furniture in the room has been arranged to create corners and small areas for different activities, and relevant resources are stored on well-labelled low shelves, where they can be seen and collected by the children. The display boards include a low area where the children have arranged a display of their own work. The door to the small outside area is evidently well used, and the area itself is stocked with a range of open-ended resources for play and experiment. A little home-made hammock is suspended from the branches of a hedge with a superhero sleeping inside; a line of small pebbles has been carefully arranged on a low wall; and a child's counting game, drawn with playground chalk has been left un-erased. Everywhere there are ghosts of the children who learn here, who have left their mark all over the room, with a promise that they will return.

Sheffield, England 2001.

The ghosts in the classroom – sharing responsibility and ownership of the environment for learning.

In this room there is clear evidence that the adults and children share ownership of their learning environment, taking pride and responsibility for its care. Of course this sometimes involves the adults in 'shepherding' as they remind children of their responsibilities, but the last thing these children and their teachers do at the end of every day is to pause together, look around their room, remember what has happened that day and decide what they will do the following day. Learning is not chopped into separate days, the adults do everything they can to join up the learning from day to day and week to week, by talking with the children about what they have learned that day and how that will be continued the following day.

'Young children are developing their awareness of themselves as learners by planning, checking, questioning, and reflecting on activities and tasks.

Young children use their imaginations to explore their own and others' identities.'

Te Whariki Early Childhood Curriculum
(Ministry of Education, New Zealand, 1996).

Stimulation of the senses

The environment for learning should engage all the senses, and the use of music, sensory materials and perfumes are other ways of making a learning environment more powerful. The use of CD players, tape recorders, pot-pourri, scented candles, and a range of tactile objects and fabrics can enhance your room and the children's experiences, but remember that, although some children live at home with constant sound and music, that sensory overload is just as damaging as under-stimulation! Choose your times and situations carefully, as you expand the number of stimuli.

Colour is important to babies and toddlers, and it continues to be important as children get older, so we should be aware that there are colours that help learning and those that will get in the way (see Chapter 2). One reason why we like the countryside is because the colours there actually lower our stress levels, making us feel calmer. If we want children to feel calm, we should take some tips from nature and use the colours we find there for our walls and furnishings, including the backing colours for displays, the furnishings in domestic play areas, and, if possible, the colours of tables, chairs and cupboard doors – neutrals, such as creams, pale greys and beiges; darker browns from wood and stone, which can give a sense of security; shades of blue and green from water and sky. These provide a natural backdrop for children's learning and a perfect foil for displaying their creations and objects of interest.

Bringing nature indoors by using plants, tropical fish, and natural 'loose parts' such as cones, shells, pebbles and leaves will increase the influence of natural colours. Resources, toys and equipment made from natural materials such as wood, and fabrics such as wool and cottons, should balance the inevitable need for introducing plastic and bright colours so popular in educational catalogues. Once you have this natural setting for learning, you have the option of adding splashes of brighter colour with fabrics and cushions, to create areas for more active play and learning, or changing the feel or function of a particular area.

Space

Space becomes an increasing issue as children move from three to six. Spaces for children in the early years of schooling are often much smaller than those for babies and toddlers. This is becoming a problem world-wide, as governments attempt to save money by reducing or even abandoning the recommended spaces for children of different ages.

'A study of the regulations relating to outdoor space in children's services, carried out by Children in Europe, revealed that many countries have no requirement or recommendation that would ensure every child attending an early years service, would have access to the outdoor space they need.'

'Making space: architecture and design for young children',
Children in Europe: Issue 8 (Children in Scotland, 2005).

Many schools are working in buildings that were never meant to accommodate an active curriculum for young children. Fifty years ago, when classes in many countries were bigger than they are today, schools were designed to accommodate children who were mainly sitting down and only went outside for formal recreational breaks. Most countries now have very varied accommodation for early learning, and although the curriculum has changed in some countries to respond to the emerging scientific evidence, the investment in building programmes often lags behind the needs of the children who currently inhabit them.

Adults need to be imaginative and adaptable as some spaces are not ideal.

Teachers who work in these less-than-ideal rooms are inventive and flexible, and they need to be! Some have no adjacent outdoor space, and others have no outdoor space at all; some are working in very small rooms where an active curriculum for up to 30 children is a real challenge (the second example above is one of these); some schools retain a view that every child should have their own desk and chair; others provide unsuitably inflexible furniture that looks good in catalogues but takes up space and can only be used for one thing, and by two children at a time. The introduction of technology such as interactive whiteboards or computers has brought rewards, but these are not always helpful to flexibility in the room.

However, the creative use of low-level screens, pieces of furniture that serve more than one purpose, such as low storage units, and reducing the number of chairs in a room can help to provide more space for children who often like to learn lying down, sitting on a cushion or standing up. Good practitioners are always coming up with innovative ideas such as constructing outdoor writing shelves at child-standing height; making role-play areas under fixed climbing frames by adding shower curtains; using carpet squares and small rugs for floor or garden activities, or buying portable boxes and baskets, so children can take resources to the place they choose.

This creative thinking, combined with careful observation of the places that are less well used, to identify better organisation, and involving the children themselves in discussing places for learning, are all ideas that have come from teachers themselves. Flowing out onto even very narrow and unpromising areas outside the room or into shared areas such as corridors can provide much-needed space which children can use independently or with 'light touch' supervision, particularly as they get older. Judicious use of builders' trays and carpet squares can make these areas instantly accessible.

Places to be with other children.

As they get older, and there are fewer adults around to play with, chat to informally, or just be with, children will begin to rely more on friends for company, that combination of attachment and attunement, that they previously sought from adults, and particularly their key person. By the time they are five, and sometimes before, many can cope through much of the day without direct adult support, particularly if the environment is child-friendly, and the programme is flexible to meet their changing needs. In this environment children will become very independent, and will seek out adults as and when they need them – the adult in fact, becomes another resource.

The need for a balance between adult-directed and child-initiated uses of the environment.

But this does not mean that adults are dispensable and can revert to washing paint pots or working with small groups! Adult support is essential, because they are the ingredient that, through sensitive interaction and intervention can make the difference between children just occupying themselves and real learning where sustained shared thinking builds on and extends the rich counterfactual lives they lead during independent play:

'At one end, too little adult support can limit learning. While play without adults can be rich and purposeful, at times it can become chaotic or repetitive activity which is 'hands-on, brains-off'. At the

other end of the scale, too much tightly directed activity deprives children of the opportunity to engage actively with learning. Effective Early Years practitioners will organise the time, space and activities in the daily routine to reflect the overall combination which best supports children's well-being and learning.'

Learning, Playing and Interacting, Good practice
in the Early Years Foundation Stage
(Department for Children Schools and Families, 2009).

Children between three and six need to be able to assert their growing independence within a schedule that balances adult support with time to be with their friends or to be alone. This means we need to continue to provide a range of comfortable places for small groups to play and talk, while still enabling group times and adult initiated activities to have appropriate spaces too.

Free choice

This is still the major brain-building activity as children grow older and, naturally, children need to be physically active, running, jumping, climbing, riding, throwing, catching and all the other activities that build muscles as well as minds. But free play within the learning environment is sometimes in short supply as the demands of the curriculum increase. It is important to remember that children still need to have the time to practise and reinforce learning by myelination through repetition of activities.

They also need to continue to explore their own experiences and constructs of how the world works through counterfactual role-play, small worlds, construction and play with sensory materials such as sand, water, dough and clay. This need does not disappear when children leave the nursery, or even after the first year of statutory schooling. The first quote below is from a document supporting the Foundation Phase from 3–7, and the second is from a document of guidance for all schools – both from Wales:

Child choice is still important, although it will begin to reflect the content of the curriculum for three to six as well as children's individual interests.

'There should be opportunities for children to follow their own interests and ideas through free play. Children's learning is most effective when it arises from first-hand experiences, whether spontaneous or structured,

and when they are given time to play without interruptions and to reach a satisfactory conclusion.'

Play/Active Learning: Overview for 3 to 7-year-olds
(Department for Children, Education and Lifelong Learning and Skills, Welsh Assembly Government, 2008).

'Play is first and foremost the process of a child's own, self- directed learning and as such is a process that has a validity for all ages of children. It is a such a vital component of a child's life that the child's capacity for positive development will be inhibited or constrained if denied free access to the broadest range of environments and play opportunities.'

Richer Play in Schools (Play Wales, 2005).

The commitment voiced in both documents acknowledges not just the need for play, but the need for play with learning potential. In the period from three to six, children spend a large amount of time reinforcing and enriching the learning started earlier, and most of this reinforcement is best supported in free play. This seemingly repetitive activity can appear to slow their progress down, but we should be very wary of putting pressure on individuals or groups at this stage to focus on the rapid expansion of those neural connections made in the first three years, solely by adding new experiences, and forgetting that incomplete or soft-wired circuits need to be completed first:

'Simply making demands on undeveloped or unprepared brain systems is a mistake, so our efforts must be tempered by patience and preparation until the child's mental transmission systems are equal to the task. Otherwise we risk frustration, inferior skill development, and an abiding distaste and incompetence for the activity.'

Your Child's Growing Mind, Jane M. Healey (Broadway, 2004).

We know that many children, and in particular, many boys have been frustrated and deterred from writing by experiences like this, and most of our happiest memories of early learning are from times when we were relaxed and feeling in control. Maybe that is why in so many of these early memories the sun always shines, the grass was green, adults were absent, and we were never called in for bedtime till after it was dark! In order to provide such productive and positive memories for the next generation, practitioners and teachers must continue to be good observers, protecting space, time and respect for play which children initiate themselves or with friends.

In the High/Scope system, this time is referred to as plan/work/recall time:

> 'Each child begins by deciding what to do and sharing these ideas with an adult who understands the planning process. The adult watches and listens, asks for clarification or elaboration, and often records the child's plan in some way. Planning by children encourages them to connect their interests with purposeful actions.'
>
> Educating Young Children, Mary Hohmann and David P. Weikart
> (High/Scope Press, 2002).

Planning time is followed by at least three quarters of an hour of active, child-led learning, at the end of which the children clear up and store any unfinished projects. The session continues with recall time when children are encouraged to reflect on what they did during the 'work time'. During the work time adults are all available for the children and part of their role is to observe and identify next steps for individuals and groups – skills which need practice, concepts that need scaffolding, emerging ideas to think about and problems to solve.

The adults will use this information as they plan the small-group time that follows, where the adults have selected the activities which they will explore with a group, using methods very similar to 'sustained shared thinking' and 'helping children to move into the zone of proximal development' proposed by Vygotsky as a key role of the adult. The process of observing, deciding what the observations tell us, and using these to plan next steps, has been defined in the guidance offered to practitioners in England as follows:

Leaving children to their own devices in play is not enough, skilled adult observation and support are essential for learning.

> 'When young children are left to their own devices in a stimulating environment, most will learn through their own explorations and play, following their own ideas and motivations. Early Years practitioners play an important role in providing the building blocks for such independent exploration – materials, time, space and a supportive emotional environment.

Yet this is not enough. Adults have a crucial role in stimulating and supporting children to reach beyond their current limits, inspiring their learning and supporting their development. It is through the active intervention, guidance and support of a skilled adult that children make the most progress in their learning. <u>This does not mean pushing children too far or too fast, but instead meeting children where they are, showing them the next open door, and helping them to walk through it.'</u> (My underlining.)

Learning, Playing and Interacting,
Good practice in the Early Years Foundation Stage
(Department for Children Schools and Families, 2009).

In schools and settings where adults are not as plentiful, particularly as group sizes increase with children's age, it may not be possible to plan with, or observe every child every day, but the principle remains – adults should be available during child-initiated learning. If they are tied down with routine tasks or small-group activities, how can they know what children can do and what they need next, and how can they be available to find that open door and help children through it?

In order to make most efficient use of children's and adults' time during child-initiated learning, the environment must be set up for maximum independence and minimum frustration. Children should to be able to see, select and put away the resources they need with minimum disruption to their intentions. It is now very clear that when children can see what they need, they are likely to focus on this, sometimes even when they have not articulated or realised that they need it!

The brain seems to have a way of working that guides children to the activities and resources that will make the most difference to their brain building, and when they see these things, they will select them and work with them, often for long periods of concentrated learning. High/Scope settings, and high quality providers elsewhere, work hard to ensure that before and during the planning time, children can see the resources that might switch the brain building process on in their brains.

The whole environment will be more successful if the children are as independent as possible – active learning can begin straight away if children self-register on arrival, leaving the adults free to talk with parents and support planning time. Child-height hooks and easy fastenings enable children to fetch and put on their outdoor clothing without adult help. Outdoor storage that is accessible to children means they can get their own equipment out instead of waiting for an adult to come. If storage or space is limited, a photographic catalogue of the things on inaccessible shelves or in cupboards allows children to see and select from what is on offer.

The environment and its organisation should support independence as well as child choice.

> 'Young children are not passive learners – they enjoy participating in 'hands- on' and 'brains-on' activities. They actively drive their own learning and development, by the choices they make, the interests they develop, the questions they ask, the knowledge they seek, and their motivation to act more competently'
>
> *Learning, Playing and Interacting, Good practice in the Early Years Foundation Stage* (Department for Children Schools and Families, England, 2009).

Many schools and settings are committed to offering free-flow and free-choice activities for at least a part of every day for children of all ages from three to six, by providing and extending challenging resources and provocations for children during these times. Such provocations are often offered as a result of observation of continuing free play, and children's own interests. Other ideas for extended, open-ended activities and challenges are linked to curriculum themes, stories, current topics of conversation in the group, or local festivals and seasonal events.

Once their interest is engaged, children will often continue an interest or project for several days or even weeks, returning to it again and again when they have free time to do so. Within the classes and groups of thoughtful practitioners, several of these long projects may be continuing at the same time, with children flowing in and out of these freely as their interest wanes or is rekindled, and with adults close by to support, extend and value what they do.

Respect

This has been described as something that is earned and not gained by right, and respectful schools and settings commit time, resources and effort to ensuring that children and adults are full members of a respectful community.

It is now quite evident that even very young babies can empathise and respect the feelings of others – babies will often cry when they hear other babies crying, and older babies will offer their own comforter or comfort toy to a distressed friend. This behaviour is recognised and praised by key adults in baby and toddler rooms, and stories, songs and the actions of adults reinforce the caring and inclusive nature of the setting.

As soon as children have the language to discuss personal problems, the difficulties of life in general, and the differences between people, the adults should begin to discuss these openly with small groups of children. The early nurturing of emotional intelligence is a very effective way of building a respectful community, where race, colour, culture, gender, disability and difficulty are discussed through the use of suitable stories, puppets and soft toys, empathy dolls and circle time discussions. These discussions enable children to understand and accept the differences and discuss any difficulties openly through scenarios that use story characters or familiar puppets, rather than real children, transforming the process into metacognition (thinking about thinking and behaving) rather than naming or blaming.

Metacognition isn't just thinking about thinking, it has a real role in the development of a respectful setting or school.

Work with the children should be accompanied by efforts on the part of the adults to confront discrimination or any other stereotypical behaviour in words, whether by parents, children or adults in the setting. Clothing and equipment for role-play should enable children to explore differences and similarities between people through their counterfactual play, enabling them to explore alternative ways of being and behaving. Books, pictures, stories, posters and other images should be frequently scrutinised to make sure they reflect the local and wider community, and the world we all live in.

Respect for children's lives, their families, and their thinking should be evident in the way adults behave and respond. Praise for effort or kindness should be descriptive and detailed, enabling children to recognise how their responses have changed situations and feelings, both for others and for themselves – 'Connor, I really liked the way you helped Billy when he was feeling lonely today. You asked him to come and play in the bricks with you and that made him really happy.'

Making this sort of behaviour the norm in a school or setting fosters emotional intelligence and helps children to understand that they do have the power to change things. If everyone in the group embraces these activities, the shared attitude will naturally extend to displays, discussions and feedback to parents, which will celebrate the individual, not compare him or her with others.

Children should continue to have a personal space within or very near the room, not just a coat peg, but a space that is theirs. It may become jammed with treasures such as conkers, or filled with paintings and other creations that just never got taken home, it may even stay completely empty for days on end, but it must belong to the individual child. A generation ago, every child had their own seat in the class, and maybe later in their school days they will again, but in early years settings and classes, everything belongs to everyone, and so it should – encouraging children to move around the room, working and learning with different children at different times and in different places, but they need somewhere to call their own!

As I said in Chapter 3, inclusive respect isn't just about wheelchair access or a multicultural poster, it runs through the whole setting or the whole school like the name in a stick of rock, empowering children and adults alike.

Free access to a garden

In most settings catering for three year olds, there is some sort of garden, even if it is shared, small or some distance from the rest of the action, but as children embark on their school years, access to a real learning garden is often missing. Everything we know about the power of the natural world tells us that daily access to the outdoor environment is a right for every child. It should not just be a prize for the few, or a recess time made just for exercise and not for learning.

Older children need learning gardens too, and they may have similar features, but these are used in many different ways to move learning forward.

Again, innovative and imaginative settings and schools have responded magnificently to this challenge as they become convinced that gardens are important to children of all ages, and even to adults. Fencing off some of the playground, digging up tarmac surfaces, opening new doors and windows in classroom walls, and annexing part of a football field are all responses adopted by enlightened managers of settings and schools. Many of these make spaces that are available to the older children as well.

Courtyards, sensory gardens, vegetable plots, and Forest School work have all enriched the lives of children throughout the primary age range, and their benefits are apparent to everyone involved. *The Learning Outside the Classroom Manifesto* for English schools supports the move with this powerful commitment:

> 'There is strong evidence that good quality learning outside the classroom adds much value to classroom learning. It can lead to a deeper understanding of the concepts that span traditional subject boundaries and which are frequently difficult to teach effectively using classroom methods alone.'
>
> *Learning Outside the Classroom Manifesto* (Department for Children Schools and Families, 2006).

Children of all ages love being out of doors, and some children between three and six only really come alive when they can take their learning outside. Despite such guidance as that quoted above, outdoor experience often becomes constrained by the demands of the curriculum as children get older and there is more pressure for a homogeneous approach that seems to rely more on teaching and less on learning.

However, the practitioner/teacher has a real responsibility to meet the needs of all children, and it is evident everywhere that some children, and boys in particular, really benefit from having some of their learning time out of doors. There are many reasons why boys in particular need to be outdoors. Most boys have a greater muscle bulk than girls, and this, associated with more red blood cells and higher levels of testosterone, mean that physical activity is a very important part of every boy's day, not just at times when teachers decide, but when they need to learn through and in movement.

If you watch boys you can't help noticing that many of them are constantly on the move, even when they are listening to a story or concentrating on something that **There is a natural progression in play, but children will often return to earlier stages if they are under stress or in new situations.**

interests them – and when they are frustrated, bored or made to sit still, the movement appears to get even more pronounced, whether this is just 'jiggling' or gazing elsewhere, or interrupting with comments that are very relevant to them, but have absolutely no connection with the conversation or the activity going on around them.

The progression of play

During their development children pass through different stages of play, often demonstrating several stages at once, or returning to a previous stage when they are under pressure or in a new situation. The progression of play in young children is generally accepted as:

- **Solitary play:** children are absorbed in their own activities, almost always playing alone, with little interaction with other children.
- **Spectator play:** children watch others, and don't usually join in or even play near the other children.
- **Parallel play:** the child plays alongside other children. It may appear that children are playing together but on closer observation it becomes obvious that they are playing separately.
- **Partnership/associative play:** children play together, interaction between individuals is developing and they enjoy playing the same games with the same activities and equipment.
- **Cooperative/group play:** children play in group situation, often following rules and complex agreements; the play will be often be prolonged, intricate and detailed.

Key constituents of gardens for older children

So what are the key constituents of learning gardens for older children, who may be operating at all of the stages described above? Of course this garden will have many features and resources in common with gardens for younger children – those kindergartens which still support most three year olds and many four year olds. One key constituent of continuing learning through play is the provision of those 'loose parts' – flexible, often free or found items that have many uses (see page 46).

Physical play

By the time children are five or six, the large, fixed climbing apparatus and the wheeled toys may be less common, and physical play needs may only be met though highly structured gym or physical education lessons or in team games and sports. Although these have an important contribution to make to children's development and social awareness, some children may find such lessons very stressful. These individuals, perhaps because they are still at an earlier stage of development, younger in their year group, or not very adept in physical skills, may feel so much pressure in these tightly-structured sessions that they are turned against sport for the rest of their lives!

Balance of activities

As in all areas of the curriculum, teacher/practitioners need to ensure a balance between activities led by adults and those which children choose themselves, by providing plenty of physical opportunities in gardens for three to seven year olds. The document *Play/Active Learning, Overview for 3 to 7-year-olds* (Welsh Assembly Government, 2008) gives detailed guidance on these different stages through case studies and observations of children across this age range.

Some key components of good outdoor provision.

Play Wales gives us this helpful list of the types of play that children of all ages should have access to in school gardens and outdoor areas, and this might be a helpful schedule to use when evaluating current spaces and designing new ones:

- 'exploring, and investigating the natural world
- building, digging and demolishing
- climbing, jumping, balancing
- playing round, behind, over, through and under
- creating
- fantasy, social play and make believe
- the elements – earth, air, fire and water.'

Richer Play in Schools (Play Wales, 2005).

All the experiences enjoyed by younger children can and should continue – from watching wildlife to digging, planting, climbing and the ever-present counterfactual role-play. As children get older the garden can become a place for scientific experiment, weather watching, building more permanent structures, fruit and vegetable gardening and ecological awareness, reaching out from the learning garden into the community and to the world beyond.

Resources

Once you have managed to secure an appropriate place for a garden, the resources there do not need to cost much, they just take a bit of time to collect, but bargain shops, rummage sales, sympathetic shopkeepers and appeals to parents can all be helpful in augmenting a small amount of official spending. Making adaptations to a garden or outdoor space provides a great opportunity for involving parents, allotment owners and local garden centres through weekend planting and gardening events and plant sharing.

Some of the events that encourage dads to be involved as well, such as 'Lads and Dads' days have resulted in really successful outdoor areas where fathers have been able to offer help in areas such as paving, structures and layout, where they may feel more confident! And of course, the increasing involvement of the community will both encourage the use of your setting by others and hopefully, more use of the community for the children as they explore parks, gardens and other public spaces in the locality.

Supportive adults

Teachers and other adults who are enthusiastic gardeners, who enjoy being outside, and have an adventurous nature are essential elements of effective outdoor learning. Settings and schools should endeavour to appoint staff who can enthuse the children in their use and enjoyment of the outdoor environment. Supportive and professional adults are one of the most important resources available to children of all ages. Their role may change according to circumstances and the age or immediate needs of the child.

Children's development

Children between three and six present a particular challenge to adults. During this age range, children become increasingly independent, and it would be easy to assume that they need adults less and less. The educational model assumes this, as the adult/child ratio in groups changes with age, but experts in brain and child development are telling us something different.

Younger children need more physical care – in feeding, changing, learning to walk and talk, and generally managing their lives; they also need more support in emotional and social development as they begin to relate to others. We would all accept that the surrogate parent that many childcare practitioners assume is as complex as parenting itself. However, just because children can walk, talk, feed themselves and take care of their personal hygiene needs (mostly), this does not mean they are in any way ready to take on the world alone. And as they stand on the threshold of babyhood, looking out into the wide world, they may seem capable and confident, but we know they are far from this.

Their cries of 'Leave me! I can do it!' are only followed by the triumphant 'I did it!' when they have the support of adults who have nurtured their skills alongside their independence. It takes **Adults who work with this age range need to be knowledgeable about child development and new research into how children learn.** skilled adults to do this, confident that children still have secure feelings of attachment that enable them to feel safe in their new independence, and a continuing commitment to attunement, knowing individuals well and responding to their needs.

'It is essential that practitioners working with children have an understanding of child development and the needs of children. By observing children carefully to note their progress, involvement and enjoyment, as well as focusing on the attainment of predetermined outcomes, practitioners should be able to plan a more appropriate curriculum that supports children's development according to individual needs.'

Observing Children (Welsh Assembly Government, 2008).

In big groups, this is a complex, time consuming and sometimes frustrating task for teachers and other professionals, who have the task of tracking every child in their group and attempting to provide what they need. But this is also the most exciting time in young lives, where trust and optimism are still alive, learning is exciting, and new ideas and activities still spark the brain cells into action, firing on all cylinders.

Three to six year olds still have the magical ability to see the best in every new person or experience as they boldly say 'Come and see what we're doing' or 'I'll have a go!'. They can still suspend disbelief as they listen to a story, have a conversation with a puppet, or lie on the grass to peep into a miniature world of ants and spiders. They can still enter the land of counterfactual, make-believe play without self-consciousness, able to be a full blown superhero, a rabbit or a mermaid; still able to delight us with their versions of their parents, of TV stars, or even of us, and still able to fashion everyday 'loose parts' into treasure, telescopes, or tea-parties.

In these years, adults must recognise their need to be independent and dependent, socially aware and innocent, mature and immature, and often at the same time. These children are practising being adults, and high quality adult models are vital if they are to emerge from their early years as the confident, open minded, thoughtful young people, ready for the next stage of their lives, not by over-preparation but by a full and appropriate early childhood.

> 'Practitioners have a key role in building the right conditions for learning. Firstly and fundamentally, adults ensure that children feel known and valued as individuals, safe and cared for. Their own rate of development is respected, so that children are not rushed but are supported in ways that are right for each child. Children's time must be managed so that they have the opportunity to become deeply involved in their activities and to follow their ideas through, including returning later to continue their explorations or creative expressions. Adults manage the pace of activities, planning varied and interesting new experiences to stimulate learning alongside opportunities for children to revisit, practice or enjoy a sense of mastery. With this groundwork in place, it is then the adult's skilled interactions, which will move learning forward.'
>
> Learning, Playing and Interacting, Good practice in the Early Years Foundation Stage (Department for Children Schools and Families, 2009).

Learning how to do this is a lifetime job, but one with so many rewards!

Places, spaces and things – a place for active learning

First impressions

Compare these two very different first impressions:

The building is old and needs a bit of attention, and the gate to the playground has peeling green paint, but there is a notice that says 'North Star Nursery welcomes you' in several languages, and an arrow points round the side of the building to Reception. Following the sign, the next thing you see is a line of painted footprints leading to a shiny red door with a child's painting, protected from the weather by Perspex, fixed to it. The picture is of a smiling family group, obviously done by a very young child. Another notice says 'Please leave your buggy here, it will be quite safe'.

On the door is a bell and a notice saying 'We all want your children to be safe, so please ring the bell and someone will come'. Inside is a bright hallway, with a welcoming receptionist, who tells you her name and asks how she can help. She invites you to sit on a comfortable chair as she phones through to the head of the nursery. As you wait it is obvious that someone looks after this area; there are plants, pictures, and more of the children's work, carefully displayed in simple frames. A noticeboard has photos of all the adults working at the nursery (each with their name) and photos of activities in the nursery rooms. There is also information for parents, including some leaflets about child development, the importance of stories, and this week's 'Easy recipe for teatime'.

A child appears, carrying a letter, which she gives to the receptionist, who thanks her, using the child's name. The receptionist apologises for the wait and offers you a coffee; she also gives you a copy of the Nursery Booklet for Parents, which gives some information about activities and procedures. The booklet is also available in other languages, and it is written in clear and friendly language. You are reading this as the head of the setting approaches…

And this one:

The gravel path to the front door winds through bushes where street litter has collected, and leads to a green door with peeling paint and a hand written notice that says 'Bell not working, knock hard'. There is no indication that a nursery group meets here, but you knock hard and after a long wait the door opens and you are invited in by someone holding a mop and bucket. This person soon disappears, leaving you alone in a dark entrance hall, which is evidently used by everyone, and owned by no-one – it is full of stuff, including old chairs, football equipment and goalposts, a box of Christmas decorations, some broken tricycles and an adult bicycle.

You follow the sound of children's voices, and reach an open door to the hall, where the nursery children are playing. Eventually one of the older children notices you and pats one of the adults to get their attention, and points in your direction. The practitioner seems reluctant to leave the activity she is involved in...

What messages are being given?

These two settings give very different messages about themselves, even before the visitor gets to the place where the learning is happening. Of course, some groups share accommodation with community or business groups, and of course not every setting can afford a receptionist, but every setting can look at their own procedures and think about the welcome they give to a new parent or even to the children and families they work with every day. This impression starts at the pavement or sidewalk, where even a non-participating passer-by can form a view from simply looking at the outside of the building. Families and children get this message every day, and although they know you well, it is vital that everyone is proud and does not need to make excuses such as 'Don't look at the outside, it's really nice inside'.

First impressions are crucial. What they see is what you are!

What can be seen of our work from the outside is a powerful message about what is important to the people on the inside, so we must be sure we are giving the message we mean, and even in shared premises we must do what we can to make the entrance to our setting or school as welcoming and as professional as we possibly can. This does not mean clinical formality, but clarity and a friendly, welcoming impression.

Staff may not use the same door as the children, so it is important to take a regular walk round the outside of your building, following the paths that the public use, looking with the children's eyes, getting down to their level, and thinking about what you see. Regular discussions between staff, and getting a view from some of the parents, will help you to see what might need doing. We all concentrate on making our own rooms and spaces exciting and interesting, but sometimes the shared spaces and entrances are forgotten and become neglected.

Practitioners and teachers often use the windows of their rooms as extra display space, but this may well give an impression that you are papering over the windows because you don't want the children to see out, or the community to see in! Notices and posters on doors are often put up, but sometimes left too long, with an un-cared for and outdated look. Litter, dead leaves, unsightly bins, bedraggled plants, poorly presented notices and signs can also indicate the care and quality of your work, even if this isn't an accurate picture of what really goes on inside. Regular cleaning and tidying of such spaces is vital, even if you do have to share accommodation or cleaning staff.

The setting should have a secure place at the heart of its community.

Messages about your relationships with the community are evident in your entrances and waiting areas. Parent noticeboards, posters advertising coming events, photos of visits and visitors, information about you and your roles are all important, particularly to newcomers, and it is useful to remember that some parents will need to check your names and locations every time they need to see you. You are very familiar to the children, but deciding whether they need to see 'Miss Sarah' or 'Mrs Bentley' can result in an aborted visit if the parent has no way of finding out who you are. Even the name of your child's key person can be difficult to remember if you are a busy working mother or a shy young dad.

So, as you read this chapter, begin at the beginning – where a new visitor will start. In this first section I have listed some of the things that parents and visitors say are important to them when they visit settings and schools, you will certainly think of more – they are here to start your thinking about quality in your own setting.

Spaces for greeting, welcoming and settling in

Outside the entrance and front door	Litter free, tidy, pleasant and welcoming Clear signs with the name of the setting, phone number, and possibly the name of the head of setting, or another contact A sign explaining the security systems, doorbell or other entrance mechanisms Artwork or photos of the setting at this point can be very rewarding, but they must be current and well-maintained – a sheet of Perspex over a display board will protect work from the weather

The welcome or waiting area	A place for strollers or push chairs
	Comfortable adult chairs or a settee and a child chair
	A small basket of toys or books for children who may be waiting with parents
	Living plants or flowers, or a fish tank will help to make the welcome warm
	A sign with information about finding reception and the name of the receptionist
	The booklet or leaflet about your setting or school
	A **parents' noticeboard** with:
	  ● Names and photos of all adults working in the setting
	  ● Photos of children involved in daily activities
	  ● Daily information on absent adults and who is replacing them
	  ● News and events, such as trips, visitors etc
	  ● Information about the setting and copies of latest newsletters or information for parents
	And **near/outside each room:**
	  ● A photoboard with names and photos of all children (possibly with their families) and staff
	  ● A coat peg and storage for each child's personal belongings
	  ● A board for recent news, events, photos etc for the group or class
	Some settings are in shared accommodation, but a simple whiteboard, noticeboard or easel is quick to erect at the beginning of each session, and will tell visitors about your professionalism – remember, this is your first and lasting chance to impress.

Corridors and shared spaces	Current examples of children's work, carefully displayed at low levels as well as adult eye level Clear and helpful signs Labels and names of adults and children on doors Uncluttered corridors and movement areas, but with interesting, well-maintained displays

The children's rooms

In the rest of this chapter you will find lists of furniture, equipment and resources. These are comprehensive, but no list can ever be complete! They have been organised according to the sorts of activities children get involved in and those which practitioners plan, not according to any particular national guidance or educational policy or method, although I have referred to many to ensure that the lists are as comprehensive as possible.

The rooms for the children will be organised and arranged to meet the needs of the group, both their ages and their differing stages of development. Baby/toddler rooms will be very different from rooms for older children, and those catering for wide age ranges may use resources from several columns.

Spaces for being, playing and learning should meet the needs of the children using them at the time.

The lists are grouped into four age ranges, reflecting the different needs of each stage of development, but you will need to match the resources to the combined needs of the children you currently work with. Groups vary from year to year, and children's interests develop during the year, so you may wish to revisit the lists regularly to remind yourself of the variations from the other stages. When working with children with additional needs, you may also need to increase the range of equipment by dipping into earlier lists to find equipment useful to individuals or groups.

Each of the lists should be read from left to right – they are cumulative, and each column builds on the one before, as much of the equipment will continue to be useful as children get older, reflecting the different rates at which children develop. Babies and children not only get a sense of security from seeing and using the same equipment, they also need to practise skills and try out their learning in different ways. So, much of the equipment continues to be vital, it is simply re-used in different ways and for different purposes.

Note: some items intentionally appear in more than one list.

The room for being, playing and learning – shared and public spaces

	Babies (6 weeks to 1 year)	Toddlers (1 to 2.5 years)	Pre-school (2.5 to 4 years)	4-6 year olds
The toilets and bathrooms	*For all age groups* — Information about children with allergies or other medical/care needs Procedures for nappy changing and toileting			
	Changing tables or areas with interesting objects (mobiles, small toys, natural objects, mirrors, musical toys) Washbasin, nappy bin Change mat or other soft, cleanable surface Storage for nappies, wipes, hand spray, gloves etc Plastic bags for soiled clothing	*In addition to the previous list:* Steps up to changing table to encourage independence Small basket of washable toys Storage for spare clothing Potties Child height washbasins Mirrors Individual wash cloths, towels Soap dispensers Toothbrushes (from about two) Hairbrushes	*In addition to the previous lists:* Toilet training seats Steps or stools Paper towels	Although a minority of children will still need help, at this stage, most children should be able to use toilet areas with less supervision. These should be pleasant, smell good and be suited to the age and size of the children.
Food, snack and preparation areas	*For all age groups* — Information about children with food allergies or other medical/care needs			
	Refrigerator Bottle warmer (<u>not</u> a microwave as it warms formula unevenly) Cupboard for any medication Dishwasher (also for washing clothing, bedding and toys) Rubbish bin and liners Bibs and towels for each child	*In addition to the previous list:* Small chairs and tables Stable cups and small jugs or pitchers Plates and bowls with sides Spoons Child-sized brooms and dustpans	*In addition to the previous lists:* Spoons and forks	*In addition to selected items from the previous lists:* Adult-sized plates, bowls, jugs, beakers for children to use independently
Sleeping or rest areas	*For all age groups* — Information about children with food allergies or other medical/care needs			
	Cots, with individually labelled sheets and blankets Baby nests, baby bouncer chairs Slings Comfort items Hamper or bin for soiled bedding Washing machine, tumble dryer or line	*In addition to the previous list:* Small beds Mats or baskets Small blankets for each child	*In addition to the previous lists:* Small futons, cushions and bean bags	*In addition to selected items from the previous lists:* Children throughout this age range may still need a rest occasionally, so provision of places for rests (such as sleeping bags or mattresses) should reflect this while recognising the needs of different stages.

The room for being, playing and learning – suggested furnishings

	Babies (6 weeks to 1 year)	Toddlers (1 to 2.5 years)	Pre-school (2.5 to 4 years)	4-6 year olds
Large or fixed items	Photoboard with photos of children, families and staff Individual shelves, drawers or 'cubbies' for each baby, for personal possessions Floor-level mirror (with grab rail) Rail mirror for standing babies Couch, futon, settee Adult rocking or comfy chair for bottle feeding Adult-level storage with easy access (for changing materials) Low shelves for crawling baby access Low-level display spaces for sensory displays Carpeted and washable flooring	*In addition to the previous list:* Drawers or 'cubbies' for each child, for personal possessions Low level seats and tables Chairs with trays Adult chairs for comforting and homeliness Low-level shelves for toys and resources Bookshelf or display case Carts and trolleys Low-level water and sand trays Role-play table, chairs, cupboard, bed Room dividers with clear panels for finger painting Low easels for painting Child-height display areas, display boards and shelving	*In addition to the previous lists:* Tables and chairs at correct height Space for personal possessions Toilet-training equipment, including step to changing table Role-play screens, cooker and other home furniture Easy chairs or children's settee Book box or bookcases Higher level water and sand trays Trolley for snacks and meals Child-height display areas, display boards and shelving	*In addition to items from the previous lists:* Child-height chairs and tables, light enough for children to use 'Pop-up' tents (indoors and outside) Woodwork bench Small seats and 'toilet steps' Child-height display areas, display boards and shelving Shelves or tables for unfinished work, models etc
Permanent but flexible equipment	Room dividers Plastic sheets and table covers Living plants Interest items for ceiling areas (pictures, lights, mobiles, patterns) Paddling pool Baby nests, rugs and sheepskins Baby gym and mat High chairs, car seats or low chairs with trays Baby bouncing chairs Cots, cribs, dog baskets or other sleeping places Carpets, rugs and soft mats	*In addition to the previous list:* Bean bags or cushions Children's rockers Cots, mats, mattresses, pillows, folding camp beds Storage baskets and boxes Plastic sheets and table covers Aprons and bibs Lights, fabrics and cushions to make secluded places	*In addition to the previous lists:* Baskets and other small containers for equipment Small rugs Carpet samples Sleeping bags Table covers Aprons	*In addition to the previous lists:* Tarpaulins Small set of folding steps Plastic sheets and table covers Aprons Room dividers that can be moved by the children Carpet squares and samples Lights, fabrics and cushions so the children can make their own dens and secluded places Water and sand trays of various sizes

The room for being, playing and learning – doll play, role play, small-world play

	Babies (6 weeks to 1 year)	Toddlers (1 to 2.5 years)	Pre-school (2.5 to 4 years)	4-6 year olds
Doll play and role-play	**Doll play** Soft dolls Stuffed animals Plastic replica people and animals Puppets Hairbrushes Baby bottles and other baby equipment **Role-play** Hats Glasses and sunglasses Safety mirrors (hand and free standing) Wigs Baby equipment (brushes, dishes and spoons, bottles etc) Scarves and fabrics Bags and purses Materials and objects hanging on strings, elastic or fabric Baby gyms with suspended creatures Soft toy animals Finger puppets	*In addition to the previous list:* **Doll play** 'Empathy' dolls, finger puppets Dolls' bed and pram/stroller (strong enough to hold a child) Dolls' clothes Disposable nappies for dolls Blankets and pillows for dolls Tea set Baby bath or bowl, flannels, towel **Role-play** Simple toddler home play – furniture, pots and pans, tools, table and chairs, cupboards, Cooking sets, cutlery and crockery, teapot 'Loose parts' items (see page 46) such as lentils, dry pasta, seeds etc for cooking, mixing and serving Empty food containers Beds (strong enough to hold a child) Full-length mirror Dustpans and brooms, dishcloths, dusters, mops Beds for dolls Blankets and pillows Simple dressing-up clothes – hats, bags, purses, suitcases	*In addition to the previous list:* **Doll play** Dolls' house and furniture Gender correct dolls Ethnic range dolls and clothes Bandages Baby clothes **Role-play** **Real home props:** Tablecloths, napkins, mats Floor-length mirror Laundry basket, pegs and clothes to wash Lamps and ornaments Pot plants Books and magazines Computer keyboard Clock, telephone **Role-play clothes and props for:** Domestic play as a family Local community members such as firemen, builders, doctor, hairdresser, garage mechanic, sportspeople etc. Imagined worlds such as jungle explorers, story characters, superheroes, animals **Mark making in role:** Message pads, lists, badges, labels, shopping lists Envelopes, junk mail, stamps, catalogues, phone books **Larger props for group role-play:** Petrol pump, traffic lights, pedestrian crossing, postbox,	*In addition to the previous lists:* **Doll play** Resources for making furniture, homes and environments for different sorts of dolls, soft toys and animals: Fabrics Boxes and cartons Wallpaper samples **Role-play** **Additions to domestic role-play:** • Adult-sized crockery and cutlery • A range of cooking and eating utensils such as barbecue equipment, chopsticks, party plates, baking equipment, • Mobile phones • More hats and bags, cases, backpacks • Shoes and scarves, gloves, ties, particularly for boys **Encouraging writing in role:** • Cookery books, take-away menus, telephone directories, calendars, diaries, lists, appointment books, envelopes and paper, postcards, notices, labels **Props to link role-play indoors with outdoors:** • Pizza boxes, take-away menus, post bags, signs for wheeled vehicles, trolleys, trucks and trailers with signs, bags and

backpacks, binoculars and telescopes

- Role-play clothes to extend the range – including those linked to topic work, visits and experiences outside the setting

Story book, imagined worlds and themed clothing:

- Masks or headbands of animals and story characters
- Characters from favourite books, TV and DVD, such as pirates, film characters, historical settings such as castles or caves
- Spacesuits, underwater diving masks, riding equipment, sports gear
- Microphone, karaoke set

flagpole, clothesline, tool box, first aid box, medical equipment, pet carrying boxes, baby scales, rescue and hospital equipment

---

Small world play

In addition to the previous list:
Cars and trucks
Farm and zoo animals
Dinosaurs
Play people
Duplo people
Builders' trays
Plant saucers
Hammer-peg benches

In addition to the previous lists:
Farm buildings
Zoo buildings
Airport
Carpark and garage
Fire station (each with appropriate people and vehicles)
Train or village set
Lego people
Floor mats

In addition to items in the previous lists:
Castle or pirate ship
Environments for superheroes and other TV/DVD characters
More track and buildings/tunnels etc for train set
More specialist sets of characters and vehicles – pirates, knights, Romans, airport, rescue sets, gardens and parks, space, fantasy
Boxes, cartons and materials for environment building
Carpet pieces, card and plastic sheeting for home-made floor mats

The room for being, playing and learning – science and ICT, sand, water

	Babies (6 weeks to 1 year)	Toddlers (1 to 2.5 years)	Pre-school (2.5 to 4 years)	4–6 year olds
Exploration, science, ICT sand, water,	Bath toys Sponges Wind chimes Bird feeders Flannels Plastic containers Pat mats and toys Simple light toys Simple tape recorder or CD player Music boxes and musical toys with buttons and pads Windmills Toys with knobs and flaps	*In addition to the previous list:* Water and sand trays, baby baths or washing up bowls Buckets, jars, containers, jugs Scoops and spoons Funnels, plastic tubing and sifters Boats, animals, people Corks, sponges, stones, shells, lollipop sticks, twigs, polystyrene foam pieces Simple spatulas, spades and rakes Measuring cups and jugs Magnifying glasses (simple) Torches and light toys Toy telephones Bath crayons Sponges, cloths Jack in the box and other moving toys Activity centres, spinning tops Dough-making equipment – bowls, spoons etc Patty tins and cutters Plastic and wooden shapes Wide mouthed cloth bags Ribbons and wind socks Toys with knobs, flaps and keys Bulbs and big seeds to plant and watch as they grow	*In addition to the previous lists:* Graded containers Graded spoons and scoops Bottles, funnels, pumps measuring cups Smaller rakes, sieves Simple balances and scales Water and sand wheels Computer Magnets Kaleidoscopes Prisms, cellophane, Perspex Garden tubs Wave tubes Cogs and gears Cooking equipment, bowls, spoon, measure, scales etc Baking tins, rolling pins Washers, nuts and bolts Straws, sticks Wooden, card and plastic shapes, numerals and letters Geo-boards and bands Magnetic construction and shapes Ribbon sticks and kites Simple camera Simple tools such as hammers, scissors, hole-punch, stapler Seeds and seedlings to plant and observe Simple weather board	*In addition to the items in the previous lists:* Plastic tubing, fish tanks Droppers, pipettes Siphons Children's digital camera Children's DVD recorder Dictaphone Talking Tins Water and sand measures Sand timers, egg timers, stop watch Scales Computer and printer Calculator Simple weather station and weather board Microscope Thermometer Tape measures, rulers More complex tools such as saws, pliers, screwdrivers Individual or group garden plots to tend and watch over time Real but small size gardening tools, pots, plants, compost, seeds, seed trays

Setting the Scene

The room for being, playing and learning – messy and malleable materials

	Babies (6 weeks to 1 year)	Toddlers (1 to 2.5 years)	Pre-school (2.5 to 4 years)	4-6 year olds
Messy and malleable materials	Pat mats Messy play with foam, spray cream, cooked pasta, custard, sticky rice, mashed potato, jelly, cooked pumpkin	*In addition to the previous list:* Play dough Cornflour Finger paint Mud, leaves Gravel, pebbles, marbles Paper shavings Snow, ice cubes Bubbles, foam Bun trays Plastic cutters	*In addition to the previous lists:* Clay and a wider range of dough recipes, including pastry or biscuit dough Tools for poking and marking Boards, rolling pins, pastry cutters, butter knives, bath scourers, plastic scrapers, washing up brushes, nail brushes, sponges, rollers Simple whisks	*In addition to the previous lists:* Gloop Droppers Rotary whisks and beaters Substances to mix with paint, dough and other malleable materials Self-hardening clay Plaster bandage Simple papier-mache
Manipulatives and table or carpet toys	Treasure baskets Rattles Prisms One-hole posting box Post and rings (or kitchen roll stand and wooden curtain rings or plastic bangles) Simple toys that move or make sounds Textured toys Wrist toys Baby gym Feathers Bubbles Soft blankets	*In addition to the previous list:* Heuristic play materials Nine-hole pegboards Simple inset puzzles with knobs Posting boxes Hammer-peg toy Simple containers for sorting Treasure baskets Wind-up toys Toys with wheels Stacking beakers Post and rings Fabrics with different textures and surfaces in baskets with foil, fur, bubble wrap, tissue cellophane Stacking and nesting toys Boxes, purses, bags with zips	*In addition to items from the previous lists:* 50-hole pegboards More complex inset puzzles A range of simple jigsaws Matching games Picture dominoes Simple board and card games Magnetic letters Lacing boards, sewing cards Sorting trays Feely bags Dominoes and lotto games Five-space sorting and counting trays	*In addition to items from the previous lists:* 100-square pegboards 100 squares with blocks and pegs More complex jigsaws Card games such as Snap Number dominoes with pictures and numerals More complex board games and card games Tap-tap hammer game Five and ten space sorting and counting trays

Places, spaces and things

117

The room for being, playing and learning – creative activities including mark making and fine motor skills

	Babies (6 weeks to 1 year)	Toddlers (1 to 2.5 years)	Pre-school (2.5 to 4 years)	4-6 year olds
Creative activities, including mark making and fine motor skill	Finger paint Printing sponges and dabbers Fabrics Mobiles Squeezy toys and balls Pat mats or messy mats	*In addition to the previous list:* A simple mark-making area with mark-making tools and materials Table or floor covering Finger paint Big paint brushes, dabbers, sponges, squeezy bottles Chunky felt-tipped pens (washable) and crayons including those in a range of skin and hair colours Playground and blackboard chalk Brushes, sponges, dishwashing mops and brushes, kitchen tools, feathers, cotton balls Non-spill paint pots Blackboards and whiteboards Paste and glue with spreaders Simple collage materials Food colouring Spring scissors Materials for collage – feathers, sequins, felt, fabric, glitter, gravel, leaves, ribbon, string, foam, polystyrene, buttons Papers and card of all types, colours and sizes	*In addition to the previous lists:* A mark-making area with a wide range of resources and tools Whiteboards Staplers, hole punch, paper clips, pipe cleaners, string, wool Home-made books, notepads Easels and table covers Medium thickness pens and thinner crayons, including those in a range of skin and hair colours Range of brushes, rollers, sponges, spray bottles, trays for mixing Droppers, thin paint, sieves and strainers Kitchen tools and other equipment for printing and making marks Brushes and brooms PVA glue, paste, tape, Blu Tack Scissors Ink stamps and pads Paper plates, tubes, grocery bags Used greeting cards, magazines, catalogues, junk mail Clips, rubber bands, fasteners, pipe cleaners, bag ties, straws Sewing and threading cards Weaving frames Notices and other words in a range of languages Papers and card of all types, colours and sizes	*In addition to the previous lists:* Mark-making or writing area with a wide range of resources and equipment, including book-making materials Mark-making boxes for outdoor and indoor play Home-made books, message and notepads Whiteboards and clipboards Fine black and coloured markers, including those in a range of skin and hair colours Charcoal Oil pastels Coloured pencils Stamps and stamp pads Cut-out punches Cotton buds Inks, dyes and food colouring Variety of scissors, brushes and containers Variety of tapes and glues Balsa wood, cork sheet Paint-mixing pots and palettes Pattern scissors Batik tools and inks Paper fasteners, bulldog clips Simple sewing and weaving materials, including home-made looms Continuing use of a range of written languages Word banks both indoors and outside Tweezers, tongs, droppers, syringes, pipettes Papers and card of all types, colours and sizes

The room for being, playing and learning – natural materials and 'loose parts' for exploration, counting, sorting and imaginative/creative play

	Babies (6 weeks to 1 year)	Toddlers (1 to 2.5 years)	Pre-school (2.5 to 4 years)	4–6 year olds
Natural materials and 'loose parts' for exploration, counting, sorting and imaginative/ creative play	**Treasure baskets with:** Wooden shapes Pegs Cones, gourds and big seeds Shells and stones Wooden spoons Whisks and beaters Metal/plastic jar and bottle lids Bells Small whisks Feathers Corks Sponges, loofahs Cotton reels Spoons Keys on chain/ring Small funnels Small tins and boxes Curtain rings Beads and bangles Brushes Tea strainers Small cloth bags, baskets, mats Small teddies or cloth dolls Potholders Scarves Windmills	*In addition to the previous list:* **Materials for heuristic play and many other uses:** metal tins and lids, lengths of different sorts of chain, corks, pingpong balls, hair rollers and clips, lengths of ribbon and lace, hair scrunchies and bobbles, woollen pompoms, cardboard cylinders, keys in bunches, metal jar tops, cones, curtain rings, laundry pegs, large buttons **ALSO** Large washers Lids Knobs Laces Garlic press Bracelets Bottle brushes Glasses cases Drain plugs on chain Fabrics Wooden bricks Cones, shells, nuts and large seeds, cotton reels Small sawn logs Cups, bowls, plastic bottles	*In addition to the items in the previous lists:* Leaves, twigs, sticks Big beads Stones and pebbles Conkers Plastic cups String Nails Screws Used greeting cards Film canisters Golf balls Juice can lids Ring pulls Bottle tops Wooden spools Counting and sorting toys Chalk Lolly sticks Ice cream spoons Plastic cutlery Bubbles Ice cubes Film canisters Straws String, rope, braid, ribbon Measuring cups Wooden and plastic shapes Seaside and country objects such as seaweed, shells, pebbles, twigs, moss	*In addition to the items in the previous lists:* A range of fasteners such as cable ties, string, clips, pegs and elastic Pieces of fabric of different sizes Marbles Buttons Beads Counters Plastic and real coins Plastic containers Recycled materials such as boxes and containers, card tubes etc Moss, lichen, roots, twigs Hay, raffia, straw Paper and plastic plates and cutlery Elastic bands Objects in pairs, such as mittens, socks, shoes to sort and pair Shoes and clothing to sort Wooden and plastic shapes (2 and 3D) An increasing range of objects from different settings, such as underwater, mountains, caves etc Objects such as seaweed, shells, pebbles, twigs, moss Objects from the past to explore and investigate

Places, spaces and things   119

The room for being, playing and learning – music, sound and sensory, books and language

	Babies (6 weeks to 1 year)	Toddlers (1 to 2.5 years)	Pre-school (2.5 to 4 years)	4-6 year olds
Music, sound, sensory	Rattles, squeeze toys, music-makers, noisy toys Wrist and ankle bells Musical boxes and mobiles Tapes and CDs of lullabies (including those in home languages) and soothing music Pop-up toys Activity centres Hand mirrors Hanging and hand-held mirrors, mobiles such as CDs Bubbles Aromatherapy oils Open containers in plastic, card, wood, wicker	*In addition to the previous list:* Simple shakers and drums Noisy toys Bubble blowers Rain sticks Spoons, wooden and metal Banners, streamers, ribbon sticks, scarves Kazoos, whistles, blowers Tapes and CDs of rhymes and simple songs Action songs and rhymes	*In addition to the previous list:* More complex percussion such as tambourines, castanets Headphones and tape player Tapes and CDs of more complex rhymes and simple songs, including action songs	*In addition to the previous list:* First pitched instruments – chime bars Microphone Karaoke set CD player Story tapes and CDs
Books, language	Pictures and posters Family/familiar object photobooks and diaries Photos of familiar people and objects displayed on skirting boards and low on walls Simple picture books Cloth and board book Bath books Book baskets with story props Cushions and bean bags Finger puppets Tapes or CDs of baby songs and rhymes with some in community languages Story chair or settee for adults and children together Perfumed candles and pot pourri (well out of reach!) Baby massage equipment and	*In addition to the previous list:* A range of age-appropriate picture books and non-fiction picture books Photo albums and empty albums Puppets of all sorts and sizes, including finger puppets Postcards Telephones CDs of nursery rhymes and simple songs Story CDs Personal photobooks Photo story books with children from the setting Simple books about feelings Magazines, catalogues, pictures, clip art Story sacks	*In addition to the previous list:* A range of age-appropriate picture books, rhyming books and simple non-fiction books Simple stories about shapes, numbers and counting Photos and photobooks of babies, children, families and pets, familiar objects and places Flannelgraphs Story sacks and simple props Simple, three or four picture photo sequences Books and stories in a range of community languages and in dual languages Large puppets and Persona Dolls Pictures of all sorts to talk about Collections of natural materials for sensory experiences	*In addition to the previous list:* A range of age-appropriate picture books, rhyme and story books and non-fiction books Traditional stories from a range of cultures More complex stories about counting and numbers Continue to make photobooks and photo sequences, including those photographed by the children Story boards and flannelgraphs More complex story sacks and props Display pictures and posters which give positive images of gender, race, ethnicity and disability. Photos and pictures of faces and expressions Pictures, books, and other resources that reflect the local community and people with disabilities, and that celebrate

Setting the Scene

	Babies	Toddlers	Pre-school	4-6 year olds
	Throws, futons, cushions		Stories about feelings and emotions Stories from other cultures and countries Parachutes, fabric sheets, Lycra Wooden and card letters Picture lotto and other matching games First number games for sorting and matching	fiction Maps, plans and atlases Recipes, instructions, labels, lists, signs Simple role-play props such as headbands for retelling stories Stories that encourage problem solving and emotional engagement Picture and word lotto and matching games Number games with pictures and words

The room for being, playing and learning – construction

	Babies (6 weeks to 1 year)	Toddlers (1 to 2.5 years)	Pre-school (2.5 to 4 years)	4-6 year olds
Construction	Foam blocks Soft plastic blocks Buckets Cylinder blocks One-hole posting box	*In addition to the previous list:* More wooden blocks, including hollow blocks Carts with fitting blocks Posting boxes Stacking boxes and cups Big trucks and trains Sticklebricks Lego-Duplo People and animals for construction worlds Cars, dump trucks, buses, ambulances with people	*In addition to the previous lists:* Steering wheel Hollow block set Pulleys and ropes Planks Large sets of small wooden blocks and shaped bricks People sets with multicultural characters Other construction sets such as Lego, Mobilo, Constructo-straws Home-made blocks from packaging, cartons and boxes Ropes and pulleys Recycled materials for construction Sticky and masking tape	*In addition to items in the previous lists:* Lego and other commercial sets with wheels, gears and specialist pieces Waterway with boats etc Guttering and drainpipes Bike wheels Boards, sticks, canes, logs, tree slices Rope, string, elastic bungees, duct tape, cable ties Large fabrics such as sheets, shower curtains, dust sheets and tarpaulins Construction sets with smaller pieces and those with nuts and bolts Cardboard boxes, tubes, cartons, plastic containers, wood offcuts, paper and plastic cups, balsa wood blocks Real bricks and blocks, planks and boards Traffic lights, traffic signs, cones

The room for being, playing and learning – large motor play and garden play

	Babies (6 weeks to 1 year)	Toddlers (1 to 2.5 years)	Pre-school (2.5 to 4 years)	4–6 year olds
Large motor play equipment for indoors and outside	Space for rolling, stretching, exploring Pillows and cushions for propping Mats and mattresses Single and double strollers Slings or backpacks Two-four-six passenger carts Soft beach balls Foam rolls, swim rolls Wooden boxes Tents, tunnels, hidey cubes and boxes – places to hide, crawl and peep out from Fabrics Lightweight doll buggies Bubbles, wands and blowers Push and pull toys Small trolleys for pushing	*In addition to the previous list:* Simple climbing frame or trestle Low stairs or steps, short planks, slide Barrels Soft or foam cubes, balls and other shapes Small wheelbarrows Prams, low push carts, pushchairs for dolls No-pedal trikes and ride-ons Balls of various sizes Pull toys, wagons Playground chalk, decorators' brushes, sprays, water pistols Outdoor musical instruments, plastic bowls, dish-mops, old pans, chopsticks, cutlery Rockers Cartons and boxes	*In addition to the previous lists:* Simple trikes and cars, some with trailers Prams and strollers for dolls Footballs, rubber quoits, bean bags, cones and canes Small bats Trolleys and bigger barrows Plastic boxes and crates Ribbons Lycra sheets Simple bottles for skittles Simple woodworking tools such as hammers and big nails Hats, tool belts Tyres Crates, planks, cartons, tubes Push carts, baskets, buckets, bins Skipping and jump ropes Hoops	*In addition to the previous lists:* Two-wheeled bikes with and without stabilisers Scooters Bats and balls Jumping stands and cones Skipping ropes, bean bags, small balls Small skateboards Small balance beams Cubes and tunnels Steps, slide, A-frames Skittles Traffic signs and lights More complex tools for woodwork, saws, pliers etc Ribbon sticks Lycra bands Woodwork tools Log slices, branches Guttering and drainpipes
The garden (see also Large motor play equipment above)	Wind chimes Flower planters Soft areas for lying and sitting Bowls and trays for sensory materials such as pebbles Streamers, bubbles, windmills Mobiles Feathers Wind chimes	*In addition to the previous list:* Buckets and bags Tents Blankets and mats Carpet squares Builders' trays Small barrows Tyres Boxes	*In addition to the previous list:* Tree trunks and log slices Washing-up bowls Safe washing line or pegs and string Brushes, playground chalk Large fabric and Lycra pieces, sheets, shower curtains Pulleys	*In addition to the previous list:* Pulleys with ropes and baskets Logs and big branches Scramble nets Blackboards Mark-making equipment in boxes, buckets and belts A simple raised stage area for role-play

Chiffon scarves Canopies and shady areas Places for adults to perch and chat	Hidey holes and cubes Blankets and cushions Benches Builders' trays and plant saucers Paddling pool Wheeled toys on strings to pull Ramps into sand pits Play lawn mower Balls and beanbags Gardening tools Places for adults to perch and chat	Digging machines Waterwheels and waterways Inflated inner tubes Tractor tyres Toboggans or sledges Carpet samples and squares Mark-making equipment such as paint brushes, chalk, paint Baskets and bags Places for adults to perch and chat	Large wooden, plastic and cardboard boxes Milk crates Folding boxes Tarpaulins, sheets Tents and gazebos Basketball hoop, football goal Tables and chairs for outdoor learning Places for adults to perch and chat
Plants and animals Aquarium Bird feeders Plant pots	*In addition to the previous list:* Garden tubs Plant pots and compost Digging tools Digging plots Buckets Watering cans	*In addition to the previous lists:* Trowels, forks Child-sized real spades and forks Incubator Ant farm Wormery Bug boxes Gardening hose Small, good natured insects and pets such as giant land snails, rabbits and guinea pigs	*In addition to the previous lists:* Larger child-sized real spades and forks Bird hide Butterfly farm Plastic aquarium Safe garden pond and fish Greenhouse 'Pooters' Further experience of caring for insects and pets

'building, digging and demolishing – *If we think about the way children play on a beach we can see that sandpits are not just for toddlers – older children enjoy digging, building, and sculpting too. A quiet area of the grounds might be a good place for a sand or gravel area. An area of "garden" that can be dug during break times is also an option.*

Other options include the provision of wooden bricks, branches, hay or straw bales, crates, boxes, rope, tarpaulins or sheets, tyres and other den building materials. Children like to explore new materials and work out how to use them. We all know the cliché of the children who prefer to play with the boxes than the toys they contain. Looking at play theory the reason for this becomes clear; it is because play with cardboard boxes offers more possibilities.'

Richer Play in Schools (Play Wales, 2005).

'A summary of the literature suggests that a powerful thinking environment can be described as:

- *stimulating – containing an array of materials that encourage exploration and investigation;*
- *having spacious teaching space and being appropriately laid out;*
- *being flexible and not overly structured to allow the children time to fully engage in the investigative process;*
- *play based, allowing for freedom of choice;*
- *having access to outdoor facilities;*
- *having children's own work in evidence to provoke reflection through use of photographs and illustrations; and*
- *having a positive ethos reflected by children and staff.'*

Thinking Skills in the Early Years: A Guide for Practitioners,
G. Walsh, P. Murphy and C. Dunbar et al
(Stranmills University College, Belfast, 2005).

Of course, you could buy all the equipment in the lists, put it in a school or setting and assume that excellence will result, but we all know that is not the case! Without excellent practitioners and teachers, excellent resources can become rigid, adult dominated, abused, neglected or even destroyed. It takes good management, skill and practice to learn the importance of the adult in the environment for early learning. Chapter 6 will explore what adults need to do to understand and support children as they explore and learn from the stimulating environment provided.

Setting the Scene

Play with me! The role of early years practitioners and teachers in children's lives and learning

A changing society

'A great change is coming over childhood in the world's richest countries. Today's rising generation is the first in which a majority are spending a large part of early childhood in some form of out-of-home child care. At the same time, neuroscientific research is demonstrating that loving, stable, secure, and stimulating relationships with caregivers in the earliest months and years of life are critical for every aspect of a child's development.

Taken together, these two developments confront public and policymakers in OECD countries with urgent questions. Whether the child care transition will represent an advance or a setback – for today's children and tomorrow's world – will depend on the response.'

The Child Care Transition, Innocenti Report Card 8,
(UNICEF Innocenti Research Centre, 2008).

This sobering quote is from a UNICEF report written in 2008, and the situation can only have become more urgent as we move into the second decade of the 20th Century. More and more very young children are in childcare, and the report goes on to say that we have still not moved away from the following view:

'In some countries, it is still widely assumed that little or no training is required for looking after infants and toddlers, that slightly more training may be required for those entrusted with three-to-five year-olds, and that higher level qualifications are necessary only for teachers of older children. Such views are now dangerously out of date.'

The Child Care Transition, Innocenti Report Card 8,
(UNICEF Innocenti Research Centre, 2008).

This preference for investing in older (secondary age and above), rather than younger (early years) children has been described as funding and weighting by 'body mass', not by need. Older and bigger children get the highest funding per head in most rich countries of the world, despite the fact that we now have as much evidence as we all need to see that the early years are the prime times. Not only is high quality childcare a way of combating deprivation, supporting parenting, and enabling mothers to return to work in an increasingly pressured financial climate, but the findings of neuroscience clearly indicate that very young children need a particular sort of care in early years settings. In order for brain building to be successful, firm and conducive to future experiences, practitioners and those who manage them must hold firm to the guidance given to us by neuroscientists and experts in early child development. Essential features of this guidance include the need for:

Babies and children are and will be in care for more of their waking hours than ever before.

Any guidance on practice must take into account *both* the findings of neuroscience and the need for governments to release women for the workforce.

1. Strong, reciprocal relationships with the significant adults in their lives (parents and other family members, *and* the carers they meet in early 'educare') – **attachment** and **attunement**, or what is described in Harvard research papers as the 'serve and return' of interaction:

> *"Serve and return' happens when young children naturally reach out for interaction through babbling, facial expressions, words, gestures, and cries, and adults respond by getting in sync and doing the same kind of vocalising and gesturing back at them, and the process continues back and forth. Another important aspect of the serve and return' notion of interaction is that it works best when it is embedded in an ongoing relationship between a child and an adult who is responsive to the child's own unique individuality.'*
>
> *The Science of Early Childhood Development: Closing the gap between what we know and what we do* (National Scientific Council on the Developing Child, Harvard University, 2007).

Essential to the role of parents, practitioners and teachers is the need for close relationships with individual children. This takes time, but time must be found, and this will mean achieving a balance between the traditionally accepted role of educator or teacher, and the essential role of caring companion. In the past, good parents have found this balance easier, particularly when the majority of mothers stayed at home until their children were at least five, but pressures of modern life, such as the work/life balance for parents and increasing accountability for care workers exert pressures on both groups.

2. The notion that there are **sensitive periods in brain development**, where babies and children are open to particular types of learning, is commonly quoted when advice for educators is being constructed. However, evidence from neuroscientists has resulted in a shift in thinking, and this guidance is not as clear-cut as it was:

> '... neuroscientists have now shied away from the term 'critical periods', identifying instead certain types of learning which are subject to periods when the brain seems to be primed for particular types of input. Such periods are not confined to the early years of childhood, and they are not as dramatically critical as some proponents originally believed. The idea that it is a case of 'use it or lose it' appears to be an exaggeration of the truth...
>
> It is a response to our environment which allows the brain to fine-tune itself, and it may be subject to 'sensitive periods' when the brain is particularly ready to respond to these stimuli, which are ever-present in the environment...
>
> There are no grounds for believing, then, in the supreme importance of the first three years, nor in the efficacy of any form of infant 'hot housing'. Any normally stimulating human environment will be (in neuroscientific terms) sufficient for normal human infant development... the main sensitive periods in early childhood appear to concern sensory and motor development and those skills and abilities which humans are conditioned to develop by their evolution (including spoken language). The sooner remediation of any deficit begins, the greater chance there is of overcoming the deficit.'
>
> 'What can brain science contribute to teaching and learning?', John Hall 'Spotlight 92', *Neuroscience and Education* (University of Gasgow, 2005).

The outcome from research, although now more ambivalent about sensitive periods, does however support the view that sensory, motor and language development appear to be 'sensitive *aspects*' of learning in the early years, and should be central to the experiences we offer, particularly to children under three.

3. **The role of love** is an essential prerequisite in development, giving young children a sense of safety and security, which are essential for positive interactions, stable relationships and secure learning. This love is not a sentimental emotion, but a deep desire to be in contact with what is meaningful to the child, celebrating their successes and achievements, however small, and noticing and responding to uncertainty or distress:

    > *'Research shows that children who are safe and happy and developing well are better able to relate to other children and adults, feel comfortable in their environments, and do well at school and in life more generally. It is imperative that children's healthy development in their first years of life is supported.'*
    >
    > The Early Years: Foundations for life, health and learning; An Independent Report on the Early Years Foundation Stage to Her Majesty's Government, Dame Clare Tickell (March, 2011).

    > *'When the scientists mapped the mothers' brains again about three months later (at around 4 months after birth), some areas had grown, including the hypothalamus, amygdala and substantia nigra – regions that animal studies suggest are involved with caring for, learning about and forming positive feelings toward newborns. The planning and decision-making part of the brain, the prefrontal cortex, also grew.'*
    >
    > 'The Plasticity of Human Maternal Brain: Longitudinal Changes in Brain Anatomy During the Early Postpartum Period': Theoretical Comment on Kim et al. (2010), Craig H. Kinsley, PhD, and Elizabeth A. Meyer, PhD, Behavioral Neuroscience, Vol. 124, No. 5, (quoted in Scientific American Mind, April 2011).

This recently reported research underlines the dramatic effect of childbirth on both mother and baby, and the difference between a mother caring for her very young child and even the most loving of carers.

Practitioners need to acquire and understand the key features of what good mothers do with their babies, and what good parents do in the early years of their children's lives. Time taken to do this will not be wasted, we must take proper note of the research that tells us to be more like good parents and less like 'teachers' or 'managers'.

4. The importance of **helping children to understand and exercise proper control** over their own lives and learning. Practitioners as well as parents are involved in supporting children from their first days as they develop the *skills* they need for learning and for life, and the *will* to use, manage and modify them:

> 'There is a significant body of developmental psychology research which has established the central place of self-regulation in the early years, along with emotional and social aspects of development, as principle determinants of later academic success. Self-regulation is a concept that involves attitudes and dispositions for learning (the motivation, or 'will'), and an ability to be aware of one's own thinking (cognitive strategies, or 'skill'). It also includes managing feelings and behaviour. The development of cognitive and motivational self-regulation – 'skill' and 'will' – vary among individuals.'
>
> The Early Years: Foundations for life, health and learning; An Independent Report on the Early Years Foundation Stage to Her Majesty's Government, Dame Clare Tickell (March, 2011).

From children's earliest years we need to support the development of personal, social, language and physical skills (sometimes referred to as core or key skills), alongside the will to use them to manage their own behaviour and responses to learning and living. This combination is what makes us human – skill and will develops in all of us, in different proportions and at different ages, but *skill without will is a worksheet, will without skill is just a tantrum!*

5. **Stress hormones can have a long lasting and damaging effect on learning and development**. I have already mentioned the effect that stress chemicals such as cortisol have on early learning, and how these chemicals destroy the protective coating on connections between brain cells, impairing their action. There are three different sorts of stress –

described in Harvard University's *The Science of Early Childhood Development*; which I paraphrase here:

- There is *positive stress*, which is often short-lived, and which should be considered a normal part of growing up, and helps children to become resilient and trusting (such as dental treatment, or the appropriate correction of poor behaviour).
- The second sort of stress described in the Harvard report is described as *tolerable stress*, which children can cope with as long as they have good support from those around them (these might include the divorce of parents, or even being involved in a disaster such as a tsunami) – the vital component is the child's attachment to familiar adults and the adults' attunement to them.
- The third sort of stress is the most dangerous and corrosive. It has been named *toxic stress*, which is long-lasting, and is often experienced without the support of caring adults. Toxic stress can result from chaotic home circumstances, extreme poverty, abuse or neglect. Early toxic stress not only impairs brain growth and the immune system, it can affect the development of stress management systems, resulting in permanently lowered thresholds for self-regulation, those vital attitudes to learning, for the rest of the child's life. Extreme exposure to toxic stress impairs the mechanism which 'switches off' the production of cortisol, and a permanent state of extreme or unpredictable response, lack of control and high anxiety can result in some children.

'The experience of stress in early childhood can be either growth-promoting or seriously damaging, depending on the intensity and duration of the experience, individual differences in children's physiological responsiveness to stress, and the extent to which a supportive adult is available to provide individualized support to help the child deal with adversity.'

The Science of Early Childhood Development: Closing the gap between what we know and what we do (National Scientific Council on the Developing Child, Harvard University, 2007).

Setting the Scene

Unchartered territory

So, given all that responsibility, it would help practitioners and teachers working with young children to have a toolkit, so they can protect babies and young children from harm, not just to their bodies, but to their growing brains.

There are key considerations which should be taken into account when providing any environment for children between birth and six.

There are hundreds of books about the care of babies and young children. Many of these give sound advice on care for children, and we could easily cull from this existing guidance some indicators for a toolkit. However, I think we are now in uncharted territory! Today's and tomorrow's early childcare workers are the first of a new generation – a generation of 'educare' practitioners who are in a situation where:

> 'Approximately 80 per cent of the rich world's three-to-six year- olds are now in some form of early childhood education and care. ...in the United Kingdom (England) for example, a majority of mothers are now returning to full or part time work within 12 months of giving birth. Similarly in the United States, more than 50 per cent of under-ones are in some form of child care – three quarters of them from the age of four months or earlier and for an average of 28 hours per week.
>
> For four-year-olds, 16 out of the 24 countries for which data are available have passed the 75 per cent mark for pre-school enrolment. In Belgium, France, Italy, and Spain, enrolment of four-year-olds is now virtually 100 per cent. For children under the age of three, Denmark and Iceland have the highest rates of enrolment (around 60 per cent).'
>
> The Child Care Transition, Innocenti Report Card 8, (UNICEF Innocenti Research Centre, 2008).

In the UK, we are entering what will probably be a long period of economic turbulence, with real disposable household income falling, resulting in the need for both parents to work, a lower number of marriages, a higher number of divorces and an increasing number of children living in households where the lone parent is the mother (information from the Office for National Statistics; http://www.statistics.gov.uk). The outcomes across the world are yet unknown, but one thing we do know is that babies and young children will be in daycare for longer and at ever earlier ages.

This situation is worrying, we could become depressed and negative about the impact of such facts and predictions, and there have always been strong, well-reasoned and researched arguments against childcare for very young babies. Steve Biddulph is one:

> 'The best nurseries struggled to meet the needs of very young children in a group setting. The worst were negligent, frightening and bleak: a nightmare of bewildered loneliness that was heartbreaking to watch. Children at this age – under three – will want one thing only: the individual care of their own special person.
>
> It is a matter of balance, of getting the timing right. The first three years of life are those when children are too vulnerable, too much in need of intimate care and all it can offer, to be left to group care by strangers.'
>
> *Raising Babies: Should Under 3s Go To Nursery?*
> Steve Biddulph (HarperThorsons, 2006).

The importance of skilled professionals

My view is that although the situation is worrying, worrying will not change the situation. We must do what we can to ensure that young children do *not* lose out in these difficult times, and it is more important than ever to have a skilled and informed body of people, with both the skill and the will to replace the missing elements of the caring role previously held by the family.

The new world raises concerns which must be addressed through training and raising the status of working with young children.

These practitioners must not just be Steve Biddulph's 'strangers', merely keeping children safe when their parents are unable to do so, but key people in children's lives, able to replicate and even enhance the skills of good parents, providing that most difficult of environments – high quality, integrated early years care and education – which has previously been the role of a loving and ever-present family.

It would be foolish to pretend that this sensitive job is easy; it is not. Even in the rich nations we have a long way to go in providing the finance, the premises and particularly the training and support for high quality provision, but what is now evident is that *it's the people that count!* Financial investment in a highly trained, professional body of people is crucial, but it may not be enough. What will make the real difference is that these women (for they are almost all women) need to know what makes a good parent as well. Without this we will end up with cold, clinical care and education, not the warm close relationships that result in good educare, a preparation for a lifetime of secure attachment, self-confidence and confident self-management. This is the basis not just for 'school readiness', but for 'life readiness' – with the skills *and* the will.

A rewarding career

In her review of the Early Years Foundation Stage in England, Dame Clare Tickell identified this crucial element in improving the quality of early years care:

> '...it is crucial to address, sooner rather than later, the concern that young people with fewer academic qualifications, particularly girls, are the ones who tend to be steered towards careers in the sector. This creates a young female workforce, often without many qualifications who often end up working with the very youngest children.
>
> It also reinforces views of the early years as being easier or of lower status than school teaching or other careers working with children. Such views, including that of gender bias, must be challenged and ways found to promote the early years as a rewarding career and attract a wider range of applicants.'
>
> The Early Years: Foundations for life, health and learning; An Independent Report on the Early Years Foundation Stage to Her Majesty's Government, Dame Clare Tickell (March, 2011).

The commitment of a key person

We are entering uncharted territory in our new world, a world where parents and carers need the same skill set, the same attitudes, and the same commitment to each child. This will need careful and sensitive handling. Parents will need to recognise that, if their baby is cared for by a key person in day care, the baby *will* become attached to this person, in some ways possibly *more* attached than they are to their parents, particularly in their earliest months, when the balance between home and daycare means they spend more of their waking hours with the key person. Practitioners will also need to be sensitive to the new situation. If they are doing a good job, they *will* be close to their key babies and toddlers, they will become not just attuned but attached to them, and

We are in uncharted territory and must evolve a new way of managing early years care and education.

this closeness will need management too. Parents and key people must be both mindful and trusting in this reciprocal arrangement.

It is now quite clear that babies and children need different things from their carers (whether these are parents or key practitioners) at different stages of development, so I am splitting the following suggestions into two sections:

- the first is aimed at practitioners working with babies and children under three
- the second is aimed at practitioners and teachers working with children between three and six.

The reason for this difference in emphasis is based on an interpretation of the research now available to us on the way children's brains and bodies develop. I will also be referring to the five aspects I described at the beginning of the chapter, because these seem to give a key to the differences in approach as children mature and develop.

Working with children in their first three years (babies and toddlers)

Strong, reciprocal relationships with the significant adults in their lives

'Caring adults count more than equipment
Think of yourselves as the most vital items of play equipment in your nursery. If adults relate fully and appropriately with babies and toddlers, then the children will learn through that relationship. Young children will also be able to take advantage of the play materials and activities that you offer. On the other hand, if adults are emotionally distanced from babies and toddlers, then good play equipment cannot make up that loss.'
'Good Practice in Working with Babies, Toddlers and Very Young Children', Jennie Lindon (www.peelearlyyears.com).

These relationships, the 'serve and return' of love and life between adults and children must form the basis of the work of the key person in each baby's life. Such relationships must be a continuation and extension of the child's home life, and that is where all practitioners should start.

Above all, babies and very young children need an atmosphere of trust and loving relationships. These must now be provided by practitioners and parents in partnership.

Home visits

It has been said that naturalists, and even zoo keepers need to know how animals behave in their natural environment to see what they are really like and what they need. Baby humans need a chance for the early years specialists to see them there too! Home visits are an essential part of the triangulation of relationships between the baby, their parent(s) and their key person in the setting. These visits are not just about collecting information, although that is an important element, they are about creating a reciprocal relationship of trust and openness between the three partners. This can be most effectively done when the baby and their parents are at home, where they feel comfortable and relaxed; when the parent is the host, not the visitor and where the key person can see the baby in their natural environment.

In this climate of trust and safety, practitioners are in the best place to collect information that is personal to the baby – their favourite toys and comforters, their wakeful and sleeping patterns, feeding regime and so on. But this information is not always the most useful. Skilful practitioners are also aware of the sounds, smells, tastes and colours that the baby is used to – the background noises from traffic, human voices or TV, the textures of furniture and clothing, the way parents hold their baby, the place and position in which they sleep. These are all crucial to replicating a comfortable new version of this environment in the daycare setting, or at least understanding how different daycare must be for some children.

A baby who has been held for most of the day by a loving parent for the first weeks of their life may become very distraught when they are left alone in a cot, even if it is at the time they usually sleep at home. A baby who has spent much of their time unattended by a depressed single mother may find your attention too much. A baby who is used to constant music from radio or TV may find your setting very quiet. A baby whose home is very quiet may find your setting very noisy! Of course we are not trying to recreate an identical environment for each child, that would be impossible, but knowing what home means to each baby will help us to understand what they need from us, and maybe that is just a bit more of our attention during the first few days and weeks in daycare. A favourite toy, a replica of the mobile above their cot, the texture of a blanket can all ease the transition from home to daycare.

The home-from-home care situation is essential to children making the transition from home to daycare.

Holding babies

Babies at home are usually held more than they are in daycare. Contrary to what some will say, holding and cuddling do not make babies more demanding or mean that they make an inappropriate bond with the key person. In fact, holding calms babies and makes them much more contented. At home, the majority of babies are held closely for at least two hours during the day, and this is the *minimum* suggested time for supporting attachment.

It would be interesting to monitor how much time each baby is held by their key worker in their daycare setting. Just increasing this time would directly benefit every baby, as the warmth and closeness underline not just attachment, but attunement – an awareness for the baby that we are interested in them and will not neglect them. Both parents and key people need to understand that practitioners are not trying to undermine the relationship between babies and their natural parents, just giving the babies what they need – maybe providing baby slings, not cots might help!

The favourable adult/child ratios in baby rooms should allow key people to spend most of the babies' waking day with their key babies, holding them, talking to them, getting to know their body language and expressions, showing them things, watching for things that 'turn them on', observing their progress and how they are learning about the world. This does not mean that the key person should be holding their babies all the time, even young babies need some times during the day when they can explore their own bodies, watch the world and increasingly become aware that they are unique and separate beings.

As babies develop and become more mobile, practitioners may be able to reduce the times of holding, following the growing baby's development of confidence and security. Babies can spend longer times lying, rolling and eventually sitting propped securely as they explore independently with simple toys and familiar objects. However, this does not mean that their key person abandons them at this stage, they become even more important as they scaffold the baby's learning through talk, involvement and being a

As babies become mobile, they begin to explore and experiment. The close relationship with key people is still vital to their sense of security and permanence.

'playful partner in learning'. At this stage, the practitioner can add huge value to play and how babies' brains develop in response to talk, song, rhymes and simple games. Repetitive play or early schema play often emerges at this stage, and a treasure basket can provide endless pleasure for sitting babies, particularly when the practitioner is there to support, value and extend the play.

The environment

The environment for babies should continue to reflect home, and be full of the familiar objects homes contain, as practitioners collect and make available a range of familiar playthings for simple exploration. As babies feel the need to see and interact with their environment, practitioners should provide assistance that continues to reflect the holding position – cushions, soft rugs and other comfortable and 'malleable' surfaces which mimic the lying and more upright positions babies are in when held in an adult's arms. The constant presence and vigilance of the key person will ensure that babies are both safe and comfortable.

Security and love

The key features of care for young babies before they begin to be on the move are to feel comfortable, secure and loved. I do not apologise for using the word 'love' or for emphasising its importance to babies – as Alison Gopnik writes:

'For babies, who are so utterly helpless and dependent, no theory is as important as the theory of love. From the time they are very small, babies are figuring out these theories of love, based on what they see the caregivers around them do and say. And these theories in turn shape the way these babies will care for their own children when they grow up.'

The Philosophical Baby, Alison Gopnik (Bodley Head, 2009).

So, for babies, the prime objective is to spend time with them, enter into their world, be sensitive to their needs and show them you care for them as individuals. That is the key in 'key person'.

Toddlerhood

As babies become mobile and embark on toddlerhood, their needs are remarkably similar to those of babies, but during this period, they often get distracted by the rapid growth of both their bodies and their brains. Toddlerhood is a time of tension – dependence and independence, tantrum and tears, confidence and the need for cuddles. The period between babyhood and the 'terrible twos' is often trying for everyone, as children test boundaries and experiment with independence.

As with babies, the prime concerns of toddlers are still associated with security and attachment – the fact that they spend much of their time testing both should hold no worry for practitioners, it just means that we can now see the results of all our time and love as these crawlers, creepers, wobbly walkers and toddlers begin to explore the world outside the close relationship with one or two key people. The job of a practitioner at this stage should not involve abandoning the close attunement with one or two individuals, but expanding it into a platform for confident exploration. As babies turn into toddlers, they are ready to begin honing their skills, hard-wiring some of the tentative links between brain cells, by revisiting these again and again as they work on communication, physical skills and widening their relationships to include other children in the setting.

Practitioners, and particularly their key person, are still very important, and even though these adults may not be in physical touch, toddlers do need to be able to see you and be seen by you, celebrating their achievements, helping with difficulties and always there when things get tough. The skill of the practitioner is a constant balancing act between distance and presence as this is the stage when the environment for learning widens to offer a broader range of experiences, expanding from close and familiar to include objects, activities and relationships that allow children to build on their emerging skills and interests. As Jennie Lindon says:

As babies become toddlers, they need to explore and experiment. The close relationship with key people is still important, even when toddlers test it!

> 'Under threes need an environment that is safe enough to protect their safety, but not so full of concerned adults that life is boring and without any challenge. They need plenty of play materials, but under threes are

prepared to be interested in almost anything. There are some excellent play resources on the market, but children do not need lots of commercially produced toys. They learn best from flexible play materials that can be used in many different ways.'

'Good Practice in Working with Babies, Toddlers and Very Young Children', Jennie Lindon (www.peelearlyyears.com).

Schematic play

This is the time for schematic play to come into its own, with repetitive play reflecting not just children's interests, but myelination in action as they follow the same activity again and again, strengthening the most effective route through the huge number of pathways they have already built in their brains. This sort of play includes exploring **enclosing, enveloping** and **transforming** (playing in and with boxes, tents, drapes, hats, scarves and so on); **connecting, disconnecting, positioning** and **rotating** (in play with cogs, cars, train sets and construction toys); **transporting** (by filling, carrying and emptying bags, buckets and barrows); and **trajectory** (all sorts of tossing, throwing, kicking and dropping). In these schemas, children are exploring their world and testing theories – who said children weren't scientists?

Some children have very visible schemas, some are exploring several at the same time, others never seem to have these schemas where we can see them. However, the job of the practitioner is to make sure that the resources to explore these connects are visible and accessible to children *and* that they have both the time and the permission to explore them in free-flow play. At this age, children may often be unclear of the pathways they need to myelinate today until they see the resources, and even then they may not be able to tell us in words. Accessible storage, both indoors and in the garden, and plenty of time to play are keys to success at this stage.

Counterfactual learning

Counterfactual or imaginative learning will also take a huge step during this time. From the simple hairbrush to the toddler who needs to be a dog for a whole day, 18 month to two year olds are exploring the 'what ifs' of other people's lives. They don't necessarily need complex equipment or specific furniture, just some simple props, hats and fabrics will usually be plenty. The action often takes place throughout your setting as Superman comes to tea, the dog joins in the construction or the baby comes to storytime. Toddlers need time to repeat and repeat familiar activities and use familiar resources. Even the care routines should not be seen as different or less 'educational' than other activities; the whole day is important.

This is the stage when counterfactual thinking needs role play, and 'practice makes perfect'.

The practitioner's role will be to provide a rich learning environment where children can follow their interests. She will encourage children to engage with the resources, and will join in on the children's terms, often standing back to observe how children interact with the resources on offer, and will use her observations to enhance or adapt the provision where she sees the need.

Tears and tantrums

During toddlerhood, children are beginning to struggle with rules and the need to control their own feelings and responses. This is not easy for them! The tension between independence and control, where a child wants to be independent, but is frustrated at every turn by immature physical, mental or social constraints, often results in tears, tantrums or other undesirable behaviour such as biting or verbal abuse.

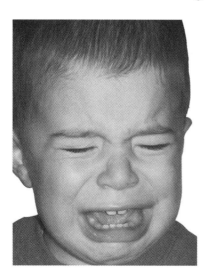

Stress is often the trigger for such behavior. Children who have good language and physical skills, and well-developed social skills are less likely to resort to extreme behaviour than those who have not yet reached that stage of maturity. The frustration of not being able to put on your own coat when you feel independent, or of not having the words to say 'I don't like what is happening', are all triggers to frustration, stress and the production of cortisol, which can trigger extreme behaviour.

Understanding this does not make the behaviour easier to manage in a group setting, but it may make it easier to understand, and this sometimes means that practitioners are more prepared to take the time to find the trigger points and help individuals to learn coping strategies while their brains, bodies and communication levels catch up with their aspirations. Providing quiet places to cool down after such episodes is also useful.

Surprisingly, these sorts of behaviours can be described as 'positive stress' (part of normal life and development), helping children to explore the range of behaviours open to them, and gradually refine them until they learn what is appropriate. It is only when such behaviour is treated inappropriately, or even worse, is ridiculed, that it can become a permanent part of the child's response for the rest of their life.

Positive, short-lived stress can be a good experience in developing resilience. Behaviours such as tantrums and biting, although regrettable, should be seen as understandable, and should if possible be taken as a sign of growth (although this might try the patience of a saint, let alone a normal human being!). They are the points where the child is crying out for help, they feel out of control and need someone to help them gain control again. It is only by going to these extremes that children appear to be able to gain equilibrium in their responses and eventually achieve that magical 'proper control' – the skill and the will to manage their own behaviours.

Stress arising from the tensions of toddlerhood can often erupt in unacceptable, but often understandable behaviours.

> 'The chief import of such findings is that it is the child's early interactions with others, and particularly with family and caregivers, that establishes the patterns of neural connections and chemical balances, which profoundly influence what we will become, what we will be capable of, and how we will respond to the world around us.
>
> *The Science of Early Childhood Development: Closing the gap between what we know and what we do* (National Scientific Council on the Developing Child, Harvard University, 2007).

So key workers for the under threes should make sure they have the support from their managers and the parents to do what the research is indicating – be more like the best parents, make good links with home, and continue to use these on a daily basis to share the important events of children's lives and learning. Most importantly, they should spend time with their key babies and children.

Working with children from three to six

Supporting the independent, active learner

'Participating as active learners within a supportive classroom community, children develop a sense of initiative and pro-social dispositions that positively affect their subsequent learning and life decisions.'

Educating Young Children, Mary Hohmann and David P Weikart
(High/Scope Press, 2002).

Although the first three years (or four if you count pregnancy), are key times for brain building, it is becoming evident that the explosion in producing links between brain cells eventually needs refining and 'pruning' if the child is to make best use of these links. The period beyond three is still vital for building young brains. It is during the time from three to about ten that the child consolidates and hard wires their early learning, both through myelination of the most effective and commonly used routes, *and* simultaneously by pruning the links that prove to be less effective routes to doing things.

Three to six is a vital time for refining and hard wiring brain connections. Neural pruning also takes place, reducing the number of connections to those which work fastest and best.

An example of this is handedness. Most children start to develop a dominant hand somewhere between the ages of two and three, but consistent dominance for all activities is usually only firmly established by six, and in some children it may be as late as nine years of age. The process of establishing a dominant hand is a long one, involving many stages: from reaching, through grasping with one hand and then both, transferring from hand to hand, holding with one hand as they manipulate with the other, before finally using a single hand to grasp or manipulate an object. This long development process will involve many thousand links between brain cells, many trials and errors, many drops and fumbles, until dominance is established. The unused routes to the non-dominant hand begin to fade away through lack of use.

Child development models were previously based in physical development, and a conviction that babies and young children were not capable of rational thought.

The simple task of establishing this hand is complicated by the nature factor which gives us a genetic predisposition to a dominant hand; the nurture factor, where parents model hand use and hand objects into the hand they hope will be dominant, and the chance factor of brain and muscle development, which may in some babies result in ambidexterity, the use of both hands randomly, or for different activities. Many other developmental lines have similar patterns of progress, and these are familiar to practitioners who have experience in early childcare.

Child development

Books on child development have been common (and very popular with parents as well as practitioners and teachers) since the time of the great early educators in the 19th Century. For many years these lines of development were central to the care guidance for workers with children under five. This was almost a medical or nursing model, where the process of 'education' was based on the notion that the growth of the body should be at the centre of care and of guidance, and activities were constructed that individual writers thought the best way to support physical development – outdoor activity, structured physical and fine motor exercises. Particular resources and equipment were all intended to support the growth of young children, who were not capable of rational adult thought.

We now know this is not true. The recognition that young children really can think, feel and act independently is a very recent discovery, and new evidence is becoming available almost daily on the brains of young children. This has resulted in a new understanding of the relationship between those three core facets of development – physical development, communication, and personal/social development. If these do not run alongside each other in children under five, then we will suffer the consequences later in life. Of course, we have always known this to be true, but the responsibility for this combined development has been the responsibility of parents, not childcare workers.

A shared responsibility

How often have the professionals been heard to say 'Why don't their parents teach them how to behave/eat nicely/take their own coat off?' or 'Parents don't sing nursery rhymes or tell stories to their children' or 'I don't think it's my job to help children to blow their own noses/wash their hands/do up their own zips' or even 'I'm not a social worker, I can't solve all his/her personal problems!'. Parents have also been heard to say 'Why don't they teach them that at nursery?' or 'I leave all the messy stuff/big physical activity/ story telling for the school to do, as I haven't got time' or 'I pay for this place, so I should dictate what they teach and I don't want all this soft stuff about feelings and caring'.

The development of communication, social/personal and physical skills lie at the heart of good early years practice. Parents and practitioners need to share the responsibility.

We must move past this stance of blame and separate functions, and accept that the role of educare will in future be a shared one for the majority of children, as both parents and professionals work together to give them combined care that doesn't only meet their physical needs, but their personal needs as well. Getting a consensus on this will be difficult, particularly as children get beyond the baby/toddler age, and embark on 'pre-school' – an unfortunate name that implies that this period is purely about preparation for the next stage!

Guidance for practitioners

The result has been a massive increase in the amount of guidance for practitioners working with children in this age group, which I have chosen to see as the age from three to six.

Written guidance varies, but most versions have common themes, threads and principles.

Government written guidance for practitioners working with 'pre-schoolers', kindergartners or 'under fives' in childcare is not yet found in every country, even those where take-up of childcare provision is high. In those countries with guidance for pre-school practice it is often recently constructed, suffers constant review and is not always helpful to practitioners, although there are well respected exceptions. Much of the other guidance has been produced by organisations working in the private and voluntary sectors or in books written by child development experts or groups. Even in England, where there has been written guidance on the curriculum for the first years of schooling for almost 20 years (the National Curriculum), there has still been continuous tinkering and changes to the pre-school or nursery curriculum:

- In **1996** – a document entitled *Desirable Outcomes for Children's Learning on entering Compulsory Education* for practitioners working with four to five year olds was published. This gave outcome statements of 'readiness' for the National Curriculum and some guidance on how these might be achieved.

- In **2000** –*The Curriculum Guidance for the Foundation Stage* was circulated to all schools and settings with children age four and five who would benefit from new government funding. This contained more detailed guidance on child development and on the content of an appropriate curriculum.
- This was closely followed in **2002** by *Birth to Three Matters*, guidance for practitioners working with children under three in daycare of all types – maintained state settings (in day nurseries and schools) and in private schools, voluntary groups, independent schools and childminders.
- Five years later, in **2007,** the government abandoned all previous guidance for the early years in favour of a combined framework for children from birth to starting school – *The Early Years Foundation Stage* (EYFS). This document was complex, well researched, and detailed. It was well received by practitioners and conscientiously implemented over the following five years.
- The latest Review of this framework (*The Early Years: Foundations for life, health and learning; An Independent Report on the Early Years Foundation Stage to Her Majesty's Government*; Dame Clare Tickell) was published in **March 2011**. The report, while recognising the strengths of the EYFS guidance and the huge amount of effort that had been put into its implementation, recommends yet another reform of the structure of the curriculum for young children receiving state funding, in statutory, voluntary, independent or private settings and schools.

So, in little more than a decade, practitioners working with children from three to six in England have been expected to implement four different versions of guidance – it is no wonder that morale in some settings has reached the point where practitioners no longer have much interest in what is coming next, particularly if it means more change. Even though early signs indicate a thoughtful, appropriate and informed set of recommendations, it is hardly surprising that the profession is not rushing to read them!

Because school starting age varies so much, and because this guidance is often very quickly changed to take account of changing circumstances, it is very difficult to generalise.

Internationally, there is now a plethora of documents advising on the education and care of children from three, and particularly on children from four years of age. These all include guidance on what children should learn as well as support for their personal, social and emotional development (education and care). Many also give suggestions for assessment of learning, and most give guidance on the role of the adult (the practitioners and the teachers). However, the different starting ages for the statutory curriculum, and the different models for management and administration, make any overview very complex. For instance, in Europe alone there is a three year difference in school starting age:

- School starting age is **four years** in Northern Ireland
- School starting age is **five years** in England, Malta, Netherlands, Scotland and Wales
- School starting age is **six years** in Austria, Belgium, Cyprus, Czech Republic, Denmark (reduced from seven in 2008), France, Germany, Greece, Hungary (with kindergarten attendance compulsory at five), Iceland, Republic of Ireland, Italy, Liechtenstein, Luxembourg (with pre-primary attendance compulsory at four), Norway, Poland (with starting age lowered to five from 2009/12, and Kindergarten attendance compulsory from four from 2011), Portugal, Romania (Reduced from seven in 2003/04), Slovakia, Slovenia, Spain, Turkey
- School starting age is **seven years** in Bulgaria, Estonia, Finland, Latvia (with pre-primary attendance compulsory for five to six year olds), Lithuania, Sweden.

Taken from: 'Compulsory age of starting school in European countries' (Euridice at NFER Nelson, 2010).

In Australia and New Zealand school age is five, and in most other countries, including Russia, China, most African countries and the USA, children start compulsory schooling at six.

This disparity in the school starting age is complicated by many other factors, not least that in the USA and some other countries, the curriculum for the primary years is controlled by individual states or regional/local bodies. This makes a concerted view of worldwide guidance available to practitioners and teachers working with children between three and six rather difficult.

There are some clear and common messages about what works and what doesn't.

Messages from research

However, there are some messages from research that can help us to confirm the things that work and those that do not, and many of these lead naturally from the needs of under threes. A first priority must be for practitioners and teachers to be up to date with recent research on why three to six year olds behave in the way they do, and the differences between them and under threes.

'Why do some children grow up to be little angels and others to be out and out rogues? Is the way we turn out predetermined or susceptible to influence? Children are a reflection of the world in which they develop. If that world is safe, full of strong relationships, predictable and enriched by conversation and good experiences, the child will grow up to be a self regulating, thoughtful and productive member of society. If, on the other hand, the child's world is chaotic and threatening, devoid of close relationships, stimulation and supportive words, the child is much more likely to be impulsive, violent, inattentive and have difficulties with relationships.

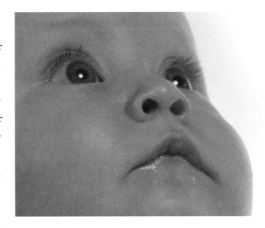

The more we create the right kind of environment for our children with good relationships and appropriate stimulation, the more angels we create and the fewer rogues.'

0–5: How Small Children Make a Big Difference, Alan Sinclair
(The Work Foundation, 2007).

Alan Sinclair's report identifies the vital role adults play in the lives of young children. He underlines the evidence that all the resources in the world will not guarantee success without the skilled, knowledgeable and sensitive practitioner. Every book, every document of guidance, every research project emphasises the importance of adults in supporting the growth of young children, and this influence continues at least until children are approaching adolescence.

Breadth, balance and entitlement

Working with children between three and six is a delicate dance between offering experiences and ensuring that these experiences add up to a  thorough grounding, which will prepare them for school and life beyond. The discussion of 'breadth' (in the sense of some of everything the world can offer), 'balance' (ensuring there isn't too much of any one thing) and 'entitlement' (for all to the breadth and balance) is an old one, and one to which there are many declared solutions. Each has resulted in a different style of curriculum. Most of these written answers to the debate agree on some things:

- **Children between three and six are very different** from under threes in the ways they behave and the things they are interested in.

   'The difference between a young baby and a three year old is visible and striking. If all has gone well they have learned a tremendous amount within these few years. From helpless completely dependent babies, young children have become individuals in their own right and are mobile, communicative, able to share in their own care and with interests and concerns of their own.'
   'Play and Learning for the Under Threes', Jennie Lindon, Kevin Kelman, Alice Sharp (Nursery World, 2001).

   Working with children over three needs careful consideration of what has come before, and of what needs to continue to feature in provision as well as what should be new, exciting and challenging to children. Practitioners and teachers need information on how young minds and bodies develop.

- Just because children have reached an age where they are relatively independent, **they still need the caring support of adults.**

   'The Teacher (in Reggio Schools) strives to support and encourage the child on the learning journey, encouraging them to reflect and to question. In this sense, the role of the teacher is not to dispense

information or simply to correct. Rather the teacher is like a tool that the children use when most needed. Sometimes they may simply observe, at other moments they act as co-investigators or scribes. They may challenge or provoke ideas through the use of open-ended questions.'

The Reggio Emilia Approach to Early Years Education
Marianne Valentine (Scottish Consultative Council on the Curriculum, 1999).

The role of key person is still important for children over three. Of course, as adult/child ratios change, and there are often fewer adults to provide the close support necessary for under threes. Settings will need to adjust the expectations of the key person appropriately, taking into account the age, stage of development and individual needs of each child. By the time children become five, they may be in much larger groups, but the principles of the key person role in recognising individual needs and differences must continue until and beyond statutory school age.

- **Children's personal, social and emotional development continue to be paramount,** and the adults who work with them should ensure that sufficient time and appropriate activities are planned to support this.

  'A supportive interpersonal climate is essential for active learners, because active learning is a social, interactive process.'

  Educating Young Children, Mary Hohmann and David P Weikart (High/Scope Press, 2002).

  This element is a truly cross-curricular issue. Time needs to be secured both within other areas of learning and throughout the session or the day to address and support continuing development of these skills, which need practising and modelling by adults and other children. Stories, work with puppets, role play and plenty of talking time will ensure that time and thought is allocated to activities which will engage children's interest and allow them to speculate and think counterfactually about the 'woulda-coulda-shoulda's' of their lives and those of others.

- **'First hand' or active learning, appealing to all the senses, is best** for young children, who learn best through play and activities which they initiate themselves.

'It is clear from the evidence that play helps young children to develop the skills they need in order to become good learners – for example helping children to develop flexibility of thought, build their confidence, and see problems from different perspectives.'

The Early Years: Foundations for life, health and learning;
An Independent Report on the Early Years Foundation Stage to
Her Majesty's Government, Dame Clare Tickell (March, 2011).

Play is described as the way in which children make sense of the world, and so it is, but we now know that play is not only the vehicle for myelination of links between brain cells, but has a much more significant role in the way children become more caring, more thoughtful, more able to solve problems and think about their own thinking. Formal teaching, empty exercises and worksheets have no place in the learning of young children. However, that does not mean that adults never lead activities, scaffold learning or use their observations to decide how they might encourage new skills. A good balance of child-initiated, play based, active learning and sensitive adult-led activities should be the ideal, and of course, the balance should always be in favour of the word 'playful' in both types of activity.

- As children develop, they are more able to think about learning and thinking, and **developing thinking skills is an important part of the role of the adults in this stage of development.**

  Children who talk and think about learning and thinking are more able to approach their school years with confidence and capability, becoming learners, not just absorbers of empty knowledge.

  'The adults' sensitivity was displayed in a range of ways in the early years classrooms. Frequently they were observed down at the children's level when speaking to them, making good eye contact and often touching the individual child's shoulder when listening to him/her speak. The staff appeared to take a genuine interest in all of the activities the children engaged in and had a great rapport with them, conveying a sense of warmth and of nurturing especially with younger, less confident children.'

  Thinking Skills in the Early Years: A Guide for Practitioners,
  G. Walsh, P. Murphy and C. Dunbar et al (Stranmills University
  College, Belfast, 2005).

Metacognition, or thinking about thinking is a skill that needs to be encouraged and nurtured from an early age. Given the right sort of support and relevant things to think and talk about, children from three can be engaged in meaningful discussions about their own learning. This works best when adults adopt an open style of questioning, shared discussion and genuine interest in the things that matter to individuals and groups. Exploratory play, an atmosphere that encourages thinking and problem solving, and adults who are accepting of and interested in alternatives and new ideas, will promote thinking skills.

- **There are key experiences which all children should have**, and although there is broad agreement on the range, these are not ranked in the same order of importance in every document

> *'The term "curriculum" is used in this document to describe the sum total of the experiences, activities, and events, whether direct or indirect, which occur within an environment designed to foster children's learning and development.'*
>
> Te Whariki Early Childhood Curriculum (Ministry of Education, New Zealand, 1996).

In every curriculum statement or guidance there are suggestions for the way the curriculum should be defined – areas of learning and development, key experiences, aspects or subjects – whichever way

the curriculum is described, there is a general overlap in the sorts of experiences children should have at different ages and stages of development. Most statements also advise practitioners and teachers to observe children during the planned and free-flow play activities to confirm their knowledge of the child, make decisions about next steps, and provide appropriate resources and activities to meet their interests and developing needs. This ensures that they have opportunities to experience the range of the recommended curriculum.

Some guidance includes regular use of milestone statements or observational assessment schedules to confirm the judgements of practitioners and particularly the key people in children's lives. These statements are sometimes used to measure not just attainment, but the child's readiness for the next stage of education.

Many of the important factors in the care of over threes are the same as those for under threes. There is just a difference in the way practitioners act.

The crucial role of the adult

My intention in writing this chapter is not to derail or dismiss any of the current curriculum guidance, or to promote a particular version or the work of a particular country. Many of these versions are not only helpful, but are being regularly revised to incorporate the findings of neuroscience, and many have strong reputations from being tested through time. If you wish to explore these models in more detail, you will find information in the bibliography.

This book is about the curriculum, or the details of its content and purpose, but any book about the environment cannot ignore the crucial role of the adult in ensuring that the planning and organisation of each setting or school meets the needs of the children who inhabit it. Adults really are the key component in a successful early years environment – their presence can make or break children's potential for learning and influence their whole futures.

I hope to encourage parents as well as practitioners, teachers, and those who manage them, to look closely both at the current advice from brain research on the proper **process** of learning as well as the guidance on curriculum **content** – not just *what* we offer, but *how* we offer it. This may be referred to as 'cross-curricular elements' (those which permeate every area of learning and development), or 'the invisible curriculum' which is about attitudes, motivation, personal development and learning how to learn. Evidence now shows that it is the most important part of the provision, and should reflect the central principles listed above, recognising that children need:

- *both* the security and attachment of their earliest years *and* increasing opportunities to become independent;
- *both* the skills to think independently to make sense of the activities

offered, *and* the will to apply them in every opportunity provided by their setting or school;

- *both* the independence to be their own person *and* the sensitivity to recognise the uniqueness and possible differences of others;
- and to recognise *both* the contribution they can make to society *and* the contribution of their families and other key people in helping them to become the best they can be.

Working in educare, particularly in providing excellent practice, is not an easy job, but it is important now and will be even more important in the future.

'... to grow up as competent and confident learners and communicators, healthy in mind, body, and spirit, secure in their sense of belonging and in the knowledge that they make a valued contribution to society.'
Te Whariki Early Childhood Curriculum
(Ministry of Education, New Zealand, 1996).

No-one pretends that working with young children is easy. It is a complex and demanding role, and offers different challenges for those working with under-threes and those working with children between three and six. Their roles are not competing, not lesser or greater, but complementary, each essential to the success of the other. If babies and toddlers have the right provision under three, then the work of those who come after is likely to be more successful. If those who work with older children know, understand and appreciate what is important for younger children, they will know how important it is to make a seamless join to the next stage of learning and development.

We are in a new world of educare, a combined provision with education and care inseparably intertwined. We need to work both with parents and with other professionals to build the kind of environment that will meet the needs of children from birth (and before) to around six in this new world.

I began this chapter by emphasising the central place of adults in children's growth and development, and I will end on the same note. In the EPPE (Effective Provision in Pre-school Education) report, the provision of a 'potentially instructive learning environment' was identified as one of the indicators of excellence in the environment for learning in pre-schools. I hope this chapter has helped you to understand how crucial not only parents, but practitioners and teachers are in making the difference between Steve Biddulph's '…being left in group care by strangers' and the high quality education with care that we all want for every child. The practitioner's role is threefold – know what your children need, set up an environment which stimulates brain activity, and then play alongside the children, watching and learning about them, from them. What is more important than that?

> '*What we need is the inventive intelligence and the will to make sure that babies and young children can exercise their innate ability to learn and that adults, not just mothers but all of us, can exercise our equally innate ability to teach them.*'
>
> *How Babies Think*, Alison Gopnik, Patricia K Kuhl and Andrew Meltzoff (Phoenix, 2001).

Setting the scene – checking the scene and ensuring quality

'Regulatory frameworks and audit are needed to make sure that the funds deliver what they are supposed to do and that standards are met. At the moment, much of the front line delivery feels its knees buckling under the weight of inspection, multiple audits from different bodies and reporting – to the detriment of delivery.'

How Small Children Make a Big Difference, Alan Sinclair
(The Work Foundation, 2007).

The final chapter of this book takes us into a discussion of quality. How do we ensure that the environment for learning in our settings and schools is not just good, but excellent? How do we ensure that good practice does not get stuck in the time warp of complacency or other professional shortcomings? How do we avoid a sense of pressure and overload as we take on the process of self-evaluation?

At one time, the thought of regular evaluations of provision and practice were considered both an unnecessary intrusion into the 'secret garden of early education', and an irrelevance for professionals who had been working for years, often with little or no guidance on what should happen in their nurseries or classrooms. Even where there was some realisation of the importance of celebrating success, there was a lack of guidance for good practice or examples of what that might look like in practice. The few available exemplars were seen as exceptions, and many practitioners found it only too easy to say 'That wouldn't work here' or 'Our children couldn't do that' or 'Our resources/garden/building is different'.

The examples of self-evaluation and practice made interesting reading for those who did bother to get involved, and sometimes change resulted, but it was only the advent of substantial public funding for early education that really made systematic evaluation both possible and desirable (at least to the politicians who were constructing budgets and manifestoes).

Large-scale initiatives such as the Head/Start Programme (1965) and the Perry Pre-School Project (1962) in the USA, and the gradual formalisation of pre-school education in other countries during the later decades of the

20th Century, brought the issues of quality and value for money into the spotlight. Gradually more attention was paid to having a clear idea of what an entitlement in early education should look like, feel like and result in. Even during these years, when quality became seen as desirable, taking time to define this was often overlooked as the busy life of the organisation continued, and documentation intended to support the process was often left unread.

However, the great majority of us who now work in early education realise that evaluation is an *essential and desirable* part of life, and that self-evaluation is far more likely to result in change for the better than external inspection. Self-evaluation enables us to:

- acknowledge our successes and achievements
- decide what we could do to improve
- record and make these achievements and plans accessible to others – in displays, presentations, verbal reports or in writing – so our sense of accountability and value for effort is evident to investors (public or private), families, the community, and most of all to the children themselves.

Any system of accountability has two sides, and external evaluation has always been present in one form or another. At its simplest and most

unreliable it is the 'school doorstep', 'pavement' or 'coffee morning' activity of parental or community discussion, which can provide the most powerful and in some cases the most destructive view of our work. When the community comments on the performance of their own schools and settings, the debate is often led by the experiences of a small group or individual family, and is based on the experiences of the few rather than the majority. Although unbalanced or even unfounded, this can be nonetheless either hurtful or helpful to those working in the setting. This sort of informal judgement, sometimes made on incomplete evidence, must be set in the context of a systematic reflection on practice. The process is made easier of there are clear, open criteria.

Where early years education has been formalised, either in the private or public sector (or across both), the written guidance for inspection has been accompanied by success criteria for self-evaluation within the setting. In the most effective of these, the criteria and the process are shared, often with the professionals in the setting working with an impartial but knowledgeable 'critical friend' to provide quality assurance data which is more robust, externally validated and valued by the professionals.

> *'Most of the review countries had a national system of inspection for their early education provision. This tended to go beyond basic licensing regulations to highlight areas of good practice and areas of improvement, and in all cases, public funding could be withdrawn if the setting consistently failed to meet the inspection standards....*
>
> *In addition to inspection systems, many countries had a national system of quality assurance. These systems were usually based upon an agreed framework of quality indicators, against which settings were accredited or chartered by an external validator. The indicators usually covered contextual factors, processes and outcomes. The systems were often designed to go across sectors and provide parents with a quality assurance marker and settings with a quality improvement strategy.'*
>
> 'Early Years Education: An International Perspective', Tony Bertram and Chris Pascal (Centre for Research in Early Childhood, 2002).

I am not in the business of promoting one particular process over another, and there are many ways of going about constructing an evaluation schedule. In some countries, this results in an external model of inspection such as that described in Alan Sinclair's report (at the beginning of this chapter), where the professionals in the settings feel overwhelmed by external inspection over which they appear to have no influence. The danger of such external inspections is that they can appear to value the *outcomes* of provision rather than the *process*, to recognise *quantity* rather than *quality*, to look at numbers rather than relationships, and to measure only that which is easily measured.

How much better for all to have a self-administered but robust process for looking at practice. One place to start an evaluation of your environment might be to 'hang it' on the chapters of this book. The notes and short lists of questions that follow are just a summary based on my reflections throughout the book, as I consider the sort of early childhood care and education that will be needed for future generations of children – as we face a time of great change for children and the adults who care for them.

Introduction: Taking the fish out of water

'Responsible investments in services for young children and their families focus on benefits relative to cost. Inexpensive services that do not meet quality standards are a waste of money. Stated simply, sound policies seek maximum value rather than minimal cost.'

The Science of Early Childhood Development: Closing the gap between what we know and what we do (National Scientific Council on the Developing Child, Harvard University, 2007).

We must ensure that, in looking at the benefits of expanding childcare services for children and families, we do not forget how the world is changing, and that the needs of very young children must stay at the centre of our practice. In 'Taking the fish out of water', the Introduction to this book, I begin to explore how the world is changing, and how settings and schools need to change to meet this fast-changing world. A generation ago, most children were still at home with their parents until they were at least five. Nowadays, in many countries of the world, up to 80 per cent of children attend pre-school provision, often from six weeks or less.

We need to be prepared for this new world. Begin your self-examination by reflecting on these few questions arising directly from the need for increasing childcare and the risks of taking those small fish out of their domestic water:

- Are we ready for these very young babies? Are we able to provide a 'home from home', which looks and feels familiar to them? Can we meet their needs?
- Do we take enough opportunity to find out their unique needs by talking *and* listening to parents?
- Are we as aware as we should be of the tensions (such as guilt, responsibility, stress and tiredness) for parents as they leave and collect their very young babies?
- Are the youngest children in our care getting equivalent experiences to the ones we all had, when we spent our days at home until we reached statutory school age? Have we discussed their needs and included them in our planning and documentation?
- As these babies grow, are we really aware of the implications for them of a life spent in care, however good that care might be?

Chapter 1: Misinterpreting messages

'Our intervention in this marvelous process is indirect; we are here to offer to this life, which came into the world by itself, the means necessary for its development, and having done that we must await this development with respect.'

Dr Montessori's Own Handbook, Maria Montessori
(Schocken Books 1965).

'From your own eyes and your own experience you may have known the importance of getting the earliest years right for your children. Now, as we have seen, the advances in medical science, psychology and economics all lead us to the humbling conclusion of the paramount importance for all children of getting empathy, the right care, attention and experiences between 0-5.'

0-5: How Small Children Make a Big Difference, Alan Sinclair
(The Work Foundation, 2007).

In 'Misinterpreting messages' I refer to the educational 'great and good' – the innovators and leaders in the history of childcare and early education. The needs of babies and young children have changed very little in the last three hundred years, but the misinterpretations of messages from these great thinkers and practitioners have often resulted in something very different from their intentions. Environments for children can be stifling and over structured, as we follow what we think a great educationalist said, sometimes without actually reading the original message, just what someone else reported.

In other cases, the environment can be entirely unstructured and loose when the adults are fearful of approaching children in case they do harm to their freedom – believing that the pioneers of childcare dictate that the adult is just there to 'provide and keep safe'. Even some of the faithful users of the great names can become prey to 'poor fidelity of implementation' as practice moves further and further away from the original principles until only the name is left to describe what was originally intended.

Some thoughts for you to reflect on:

- Is out practice really based on clear principles, which we have read and discussed as a team? Are these principles evident in our practice as we observe the daily activity of our setting?
- Have we all read and discussed the curriculum documents, both the national guidance and the documents produced from within our

Setting the scene – checking the scene and ensuring quality

establishment? How often are these revisited and revised to meet the emerging needs of the children?

- Does our practice genuinely reflect the good practice of previous generations? If not, what are the pressures that have distracted us or derailed our work?
- Do we keep up to date with what the experts are telling us about early development?
- Are we ready to defend what we do, giving clear reasons and evidence?

Chapter 2: The blue and the green

'Naturalise play spaces. Kids don't need much to engage their imaginations. Allowing grass and leafy plants to flourish in play spaces will provide endless opportunities for play and discovery'.
Number 27 in *The Third Teacher: 79 Ways You Can Use Design to Transform Teaching and Learning,* OWP/P Architects (Abrams, 2010).

'The blue and the green' describes the importance of gardens and open spaces to children and the adults who live and work with them. Gardens vary widely in size, scope, appeal and condition, and their quality reflects the gardeners. The difference between a good garden and a great garden is not its tidiness or perfection – that sort of perfection will remind us of public parks and signs that say 'Please keep off the grass!'. A great garden is full of secrets and surprises, 'loose parts' and growing things. It is also a reflection of the people who play in it, rest in it and work with it: growing things, watching things, building things, climbing, swinging and jumping on things. Great gardens are not always tidy, but they are always changing, always ready for tomorrow's play, or with reminders of yesterday's adventures. They are works in progress for learning and for living.

Here are a few questions to start you thinking about how your garden is growing:

- How important is the garden to us, both the adults and the children?
- Does our garden attract every child to be out of doors? Can they go out at most times, in all weathers and seasons and be real 'free range' children? If not, are we exploring every possibility for access to the great outdoors?
- Do we all spend time on the garden, or is it only the younger (or even

the lower paid) members of staff? Do we show interest and enjoyment in being outside?

- Is our garden genuinely a 'work in progress', full of projects and loose parts?
- Is that garden just as important to children of all ages, both genders and all sorts of interests, with places to learn and rest as well as places to be active and exuberant?

Chapter 3: Attachment and attunement – what do babies and toddlers need?

'Young children develop optimally through close, affectionate relationships and positive responsive interactions with others, particularly adults, but also with other children. Warm relationships are fundamental to meeting the young child's need for love, security, recognition and encouragement.'

Guidance Pack for Practitioners Working With Two Year olds
(Department of Education, Northern Ireland, 2008).

This chapter begins to unpick the needs of babies and children at different ages and stages. It looks at the needs of babies, for attachment to others and for your attunement to their needs, taking the part, but not the place of a parent when their real parents can't be there. Babies really need to feel that the nursery or daycare setting is a 'home from home' with familiar elements carried across the frequent transitions from place to place and person to person.

As babies and toddlers become more mobile, their needs change, but they still need to be close to key people in their lives. They increasingly need to be independent, they require more space and more choice in the things they do – more power over their own learning, but with an interested adult not too far away! These toddlers are beginning to hard wire their learning in repetitive and exploratory play, so provision for children at this age is a carefully balanced judgement between freedom and security. Some thoughts for you to consider:

- In our first contacts with parents and carers do we make time to recognise the unique nature and needs of each baby and their parents? During home visits, do we spend as much time listening as we do talking?

- Is the information offered to us by parents used by everyone, not just the baby's key person?
- How does our provision for the under threes reflect what we know about how they learn and the way they think at different stages of development?
- Do we value the people and the activities provided for the youngest children as much as those who work with the older ones?
- As babies grow and turn into toddlers, do we think about the different use of space, time and resources to support their growing independence, not forgetting that they still need the close presence of adults?

Chapter 4: Moving on up – what do our children need from three to six?

'Successful teachers are those who are proactive participants in shaping learning experiences and extending knowledge rather than remaining on the periphery. To help shape these learning experiences she emphasises the importance of modelling effective thinking strategies to make thinking more explicit in the classroom. This may be as simple as using the word 'think' more frequently and other thinking language, or the practitioner may ask the children to waggle their 'thinking thumbs' to show physically they are thinking or ask them 'to put on their thinking caps.'

Thinking Skills in the Early Years: A Guide for Practitioners,
G. Walsh, P. Murphy and C. Dunbar et al (Stranmills University College, Belfast, 2005).

The second part of the conversation about children is in Chapter 4. It explores the needs and differences of three to six year olds, as they grow into social beings and independent thinkers. This is when the time they have spent soft wiring learning really becomes obvious as they practise and repeat skills and knowledge, fixing these securely in their brains and bodies. It is also the time when role-play, small world play and story-telling are important as children think counterfactually about alternative ways of being and behaving.

Adults working with 3-6 year olds must be aware of the balance between intervening and leaving the child to pursue their own agenda. It is easy to damage the flow of children's thinking and learning by jumping in to help or advise too soon, or to be so careful to protect their independence that their need for company and some shared thinking goes unnoticed. It may sometimes seem that at this stage, the adult just needs to set up the environment and let the children engage with it, but children still need the presence, stimulation and interest of others, both adults and children, to discuss, explain, expand and confirm their learning, building on what has gone before to construct a stable personal, social and intellectual architecture for their brains. Consider the following:

- How do we build on what has gone before as children become more independent? Do we carefully consider the need for security and repetition in children's playful learning?
- Does the learning environment combine plenty of opportunities to practise familiar skills and activities with challenges and provocations that really make children think? Do we build thinking skills (metacognition) into our daily language and practice, so children are used to thinking about thinking?
- How well do we manage the balance between children's need to practise and perfect skills through play while still offering 'playful adult activities' that extend and soft-wire new learning?
- Are the resources in our setting or school arranged and stored to make selection easy, switching on the desire to myelinate learning through play?
- Do we understand what is happening when children play? Are role-play and counterfactual thinking an element of quality provision where children can really practise being someone else, doing something else, responding in a different way to their experiences of life?

Chapter 5: Places, spaces and things – a place for active learning

'For social behaviour, children who had attended high quality provision showed significantly better outcomes in terms of Self-regulation, Positive social behaviour and reductions in Anxious behaviour at age 6. For anti-social behaviour, children who had attended low quality provision showed significantly poorer outcomes than those who had attended high quality provision.'

Effective Provision of Pre-School Education (EPPE)
Technical Paper 12 – 'The Final Report: Effective Pre-school Education' (DfES/Institute of Education, University of London, **2004**).

This chapter contains some guidance on the places, spaces and things that might be considered for inclusion in a high quality setting. Of course, equipment can't make excellence by itself, but thinking about equipment can  lead to thinking about how it can be used to enhance children's experiences of the world in your setting or school. I include some prompts for thinking about the first impressions as children and their parents come to your setting or school, as well as a cumulative list of equipment and resources to suit the growing brains and bodies of the children.

No-one would expect to have everything on this list, it is just a start – a thought and discussion provoker, neither complete nor meant to be prescriptive. You will certainly be able to add to the list, and it may contain some items for which you have no use, no funding or no space – discussion of your own situation must dictate the final selection.

Review of resources is a time-consuming but crucial part of the role of adults in early learning. Resources that are poorly made, in poor condition, broken or incomplete, insufficient for productive play, inconveniently stored or irrelevant to the lives of the children, take up useful space and may prevent children from seeing or getting to the things they really want and need! Think about the following:

- Is the first impression people get when they arrive the impression we want them to have? Do we regularly follow the entry path of visitors to make sure they get positive first experiences of our school or setting, even if it is in shared accommodation?
- Do the resources we provide reflect the homes and communities of the children? Do we involve the children in the selection, purchase and organisation of our places, spaces and things?
- Do we regularly review the resources available in our school or setting and use these reviews to make decisions about future purchases? Does this regular review consider the quantity, *and* the quality, sufficiency, condition, storage and relevance of the resources, furniture and equipment?

- Does our regular review take into account under-use of equipment as well as the condition of popular resources? Does the review take into account the storage and organisation of the resources?
- Are the resources stored in a way that makes them both visible and accessible to the children, switching on their desire to use them?

Chapter 6: Play with me! The role of early years practitioners and teachers in children's lives and learning

'Being an effective adult in helping children to learn involves being both skilful and thoughtful. Many Early Years practitioners shy away from using the word 'teaching' to describe their work with children, perhaps because of the perception that teaching implies a particular 'top-down' or formal way of working with children. In fact, teaching is much broader and more subtle than that, and covers the many different ways in which adults help children to learn. The more we are aware of our practices – what we do, why we do it, its impact on children and their learning – and the more we reflect, learn and develop our practice, the more effective we will be.'

Learning, Playing and Interacting, Good practice in the Early Years Foundation Stage (Department for Children Schools and Families, 2009).

Adults are the key factor in providing high quality experiences for babies and children. They are the ones who can enable or restrict children's experiences, and particularly their feeling of attachment to the setting.

The title 'Play with me!' was carefully chosen to reflect what babies and children want of the adults they live and learn with. Most of the time of practitioner's time in these early years must be spent in direct contact with the children, and they need to be freed from *unnecessary* paperwork or routines that draw them away from the children. This does not mean that the adults are ever present in a way that restricts self-directed play, but that adults are always aware of what is going on, 'standing in the wings' watching what is going on and making sensitive judgements about when to intervene.

Neither does this mean that there is no place for teaching – that 'playful adult-led' activity described in guidance for the early years in England. It would be most inefficient to wait for every child to learn everything by accident, or when they show an interest in learning it! When asked how he had become so successful as a scientist, Isaac Newton said, *'If I have seen further it is only by standing on the shoulders of giants'*. He was recognising the art his teachers had played in helping him to realise what was possible, and to introduce him to new ideas and way of thinking.

Early years professionals need to be those giants, metaphorically holding children up so they can see and experience opportunities, activities and ideas that they may not even realise were possible, and might never have discovered on their own.

Reflect on this aspect of your vital role as an early years professional:

- Have we discussed the role of adults in our setting or school? Do we have a clear idea, not just of our job description, but our role in making that job description effective in practice?
- Do we value every practitioner equally, whatever the age group they work with, their own age, and their status within our organisation? Do we make sure everyone has a chance to show their strengths and skills, and to go on being a learner through appropriate professional development?
- Are we able to discuss and consider change and development of our ideas, the organisation of our spaces, the way we work, the resources we use? Is our practice full of new ideas, new resources and new ways of doing things?
- The role of the adult in early years care and education (sometimes called educare) is changing fast – are we keeping up with the changes, by developing new ways of working for the new world?
- Babies and children need strong adults – do we care for each other and make sure we are a strong team, supporting each other whatever the needs and concerns – are we truly colleagues and friends to the people we work with?

Chapter 7: Setting the scene, checking the scene: ensuring quality

'With few exceptions, people choose to work with young children because they like them, enjoy their company and are interested in seeing them grow and develop.'

People Under Three, Elinor Goldschmeid and Sonia Jackson
(Routledge, 1994).

Liking children and being interested in them is an absolute essential for excellent practice, but it is not enough in itself. Without self-examination we are lost in the undergrowth of care without quality, and that could result in care of the worst sort – 'group care with strangers' as described by Steve Biddulph.

It is the responsibility of each one of us to reflect on our own practice, and the responsibility of our managers to recognise our strengths and needs, just as practitioners respond to the strengths and needs of babies and young children. In this chapter I have suggested some questions for your consideration when reflecting on the environment for learning. These questions can only be a starting point in your work – the immediate responses you make as you read the questions will be from your heart, but secure evidence needs much more! You will, of course, need to add to your first responses by asking colleagues, parents and children for their comments, observing practice in your setting or school, looking at the documentation and in particular evaluating the quality of the environment for learning.

In England, there is now an emphasis on both external and in-house evaluation of quality. An extensive system of external inspection exists, having been amended and simplified over nearly two decades since its establishment in 1992. The Framework for OFSTED inspections is now a public document and has been re-written many times in efforts to clarify the criteria and make these more applicable in practice. Schools (and more recently, settings in educare) are now encouraged to take account of these criteria in their internal evaluations.

However, the criteria I have included as a final set of questions was first used as the basis for research in the Effective Provision in Pre-school Education (EPPE) project, which has now been running in England for a number of years. These six questions have stood the test of time, and could form a valid starting point in any setting for a more extensive process of self-evaluation, and I recommend them as a starting point for you:

- 'How can I improve the 'quality' of my pre-school setting?
- To what extent does our pre-school setting engage children in 'sustained shared thinking'?
- How do we ensure that staff have in-depth knowledge and understanding of an appropriate early years curriculum?
- What do we know about how children learn?
- How do we support children in resolving conflicts?
- How do we help parents to support children's learning in the home?'

> *Assessing Quality in the Early Years: Early Childhood Environment Rating Scale* (ECERS-E); Kathy Sylva, Iram Siraj-Blatchford and Brenda Taggart (**Trentham Books, 2003**).

Quality early years provision will be essential if we are to meet the future needs of the children who will work for us, look to us for inspiration, and care for us as we grow old:

> *'The children starting kindergarten this fall will graduate in the third decade of the 21st Century. All we can know about the world she will step into is that it will have challenges and opportunities beyond what we can imagine today, problems and possibilities that will demand creativity and ingenuity, responsibility and compassion. Whether this year's kindergarten student will merely survive or positively thrive in the decades to come depends in large measure on the experiences she has in school.'*

> *The Third Teacher: 79 Ways You Can Use Design to Transform Teaching and Learning,* OWP/P Architects (Abrams, 2010).

I hope we will be able to live up to their expectations!

Postscript

As I was in the final stages of completing this book, there was a flurry of new evidence on the current state of well-being of children in the UK and across Europe, and a further flurry of responses to the international financial situation affecting government funding for new and existing initiatives.

Doing better for families

The most far-reaching of these was the OECD (Organisation for Economic and Cultural Development) report, *Doing Better for Families* (2011), which built on previous reports including the OECD report, *Doing Better for Children* (2009). This report was concerned with the way OECD countries are tacking poverty and addressing the needs of families, particularly those with children, and the findings echo many of the issues covered in this book:

> *'Families are the cornerstone of society and play an important role in the economy. Families are a key source of financial and social support for the vast majority of people. They are a crucial engine of solidarity: redistributing resources – in cash, in kind and in time – among individuals, households, and generations, providing protection and insurance against economic loss and hardship...'*
>
> *Doing Better for Families* (OECD, 2011).

The best childcare provision cannot hope to replace the role of the family in society and in the lives of individual children. However, the world is changing, and the word 'family' describes many different relationships, with parents increasingly under pressure to work and to find quality care for their children. Such care should be of the highest quality possible, where children can find both refuge and enjoyment in a setting where there are features of the best sort of home – love, physical contact, and space to play with other children in the company of highly skilled and caring adults:

> *'Parents are under pressure to combine work and family commitments, and policy needs to support families in the areas of financial support,*

parental leave, formal care arrangements and flexible workplace practices.... Childcare is particularly important for reconciling work and family life. Parents are more likely to be in work and be more productive and happy in work if childcare is accessible, affordable, and they are confident that their children are being looked after properly.... Some evidence suggests that low-quality care, long hours in care, and enrolment before age one is associated with behavioural problems in children. By contrast, high – quality formal childcare is linked with cognitive and developmental gains, particularly for children from more disadvantaged home environments...'

Doing Better for Families (OECD, 2011).

Protecting the vulnerable

It is now very clear that when making priorities for childcare provision governments should be particularly mindful of vulnerable children and their families, and should ensure that settings are funded and staffed so they can support parents and children together. Such provision has been successfully implemented in the UK through the network of nearly 4,000 Sure Start children's centres:

'In the context of fiscal consolidation, authorities should aim to ensure that spending on children during their early years is protected from large "austerity cuts", and that overall, the most vulnerable families are protected. Public spending on family benefits and in-kind services should be seen as investment for the future.'

Doing Better for Families (OECD, 2011).

However, in some countries, and particularly in the UK, the quality of provision is now under threat. The Sure Start programme was evaluated in 2010, and the cross-party committee of the House of Commons came to the following conclusion:

'The Sure Start programme as a whole is one of the most innovative and ambitious Government initiatives of the past two decades. We have heard almost no negative comment about its intentions and principles; it has been solidly based on evidence that the early years are when the greatest difference can be made to a child's life chances, and in many areas it has successfully cut through the silos that so often bedevil public service delivery. Children's Centres are a substantial

investment with a sound rationale, and it is vital that this investment is allowed to bear fruit over the long term.'

House of Commons; Children, Schools and Families Committee:
Sure Start Children's Centres, Fifth Report of Session 2009–10
(The Stationery Office, 2010).

Soon after the UK General Election in 2010, the Coalition government committed itself to looking closely at all government funding, particularly in the public sector, and to reduce spending by targeting what they perceive to be areas of excessive investment. Their commitment to continuing the reduction in child poverty was welcomed by everyone, and there was hope that the Sure Start programme would be protected. However, despite a promise to retain funding for Sure Start centres, the latest Child Poverty Act (2011) did not build on the acknowledged successes of work done in previous years and the commitments agreed in the Child Poverty Act 2010, particularly in reflecting the recommendations of the House of Commons Report on the successes of Sure Start children's centres, such as those relating to qualified staff:

'We recommend that the Government investigate the need for a qualification specific to Children's Centre outreach work, based on the experiences of long-standing Centres with a track record of success in engaging vulnerable families.'

House of Commons; Children, Schools and Families Committee:
Sure Start Children's Centres, Fifth Report of Session 2009–10
(The Stationery Office, 2010).

The new government, in their proposals *A New Approach to Child Poverty* (The Child Poverty Act 2011), clearly laid out the following:

'We welcome his (Frank Fields) recommendation that national and local government should give greater prominence to the earliest years in life, establishing the early or "Foundation Years" as of equal status and importance as primary and secondary school years, and increasing public understanding of how babies and young children develop and what is important to ensure their healthy progress in this crucial period.

We have maintained funding for Sure Start Children's Centres, as part of the Early Intervention Grant.'

A New Approach to Child Poverty: Tackling the Causes of Disadvantage and Transforming Families' Lives (HM Government; Department for Work and Pensions and Department for Education, 2011).

Budget cuts

At the same time, the government moved swiftly to reduce the budgets of local authorities, removing the ring-fencing protecting children's centre funding, and particularly the budgets for trained and experienced staff essential to the continuation of this initiative. Local authorities have been given the responsibility (and the blame) for making difficult decisions on how cuts can be managed, particularly for the most vulnerable in society. The effect has resulted in a substantial reduction nationally, and the decimation in some authorities, of key Sure Start staff.

The government has suggested that the highly trained and experienced staff who were in the past able to support parents and families in parenting skills, financial management, training for work, and dealing with social issues such as debt and family breakdown, can be replaced by well meaning, but often untrained and inexperienced people from the local community (the Big Society), or from charities, which are also experiencing a great reduction in their funds. It is difficult to believe that this can happen without a huge impact on children's lives.

Improving child poverty levels

The OECD report on Child Poverty; *Doing Better for Families* (2011) noted that an increase in investment in services for families between 1995 and 2005 had resulted in a greater fall in child poverty levels in the UK than in any other OECD country, but such investment could easily be undermined:

> *'Progress in child poverty reduction in the UK has stalled, and is now predicted to increase, and so social protection on families – particularly via family service provisions, as a longer-term solution to poverty risks – needs to be protected.'*
>
> *Doing Better for Families* (OECD, 2011).

Political imperatives following an election often result in new directions, and of course most countries in the world are facing financial difficulties, but it would be a real backward step if initiatives that are obviously successful, such as children's centres, and particularly those focusing on the well-being of children and families, are at risk.

Commitment to quality

Readers of this book will already be familiar with the effects of early childhood experiences on the long-term development of children. We now need to underpin our commitment to quality with an understanding of the changing needs of parents and wider society, ensuring that the environment for learning reflects the best elements of both home and childcare, after all, this investment is for all our futures.

> '*The future of any society depends on its ability to foster the health and well-being of the next generation. Stated simply, today's children will become tomorrow's citizens, workers, and parents. When we invest wisely in children and families, the next generation will pay that back through a lifetime of productivity and responsible citizenship. When we fail to provide children with what they need to build a strong foundation for healthy and productive lives, we put our future prosperity and security at risk.*'
>
> *The Science of Early Childhood Development: Closing the gap between what we know and what we do* (National Scientific Council on the Developing Child, Harvard University, 2007). http://www.developingchild.net

Bibliography and further reading

Allen, Graham; *Early Intervention: The Next Steps*; HM Government; January 2011

Ball, Sir Christopher; *Start Right; The Importance of Early Learning*; Royal Society of Arts; 1994.

Bergstrom Matti, Emeritus professor of neurophysiology at the University of Helsinki; in 'Children in Europe'; 2005

Bertram, Tony and Pascal, Chris; 'Early Years Education: An International Perspective'; Centre for Research in Early Childhood; Birmingham; 2002

Biddulph, Steve; *Raising Babies: Should Under 3s Go To Nursery?* HarperThorsons, London, 2006.

Brosterman, Norman; *Inventing Kindergarten*; Abrams; 1997

Children in Europe Issue 8 – 'Making space: architecture and design for young children'; from Children in Scotland; 2005

Curriculum for Excellence, Scotland; Learning and Teaching Scotland, 2010

Department for Children, Education and Lifelong Learning and Skills; *Play/Active Learning: Overview for 3 to 7-year-olds*; Welsh Assembly Government; 2008

Department for Children Schools and Families; *Learning Outside the Classroom Manifesto*; 2006).

Department for Children Schools and Families; *Learning, Playing and Interacting: Good practice in the Early Years Foundation Stage*; 2009

Department for Education; *Desirable Outcomes for Children's Learning on Entering Compulsory Education*; SCAA; 1996

Department for Education and Skills; *Practice Guidance for the Early Years Foundation Stage*; 2007.

Department of Education, Northern Ireland; *Guidance Pack for Practitioners working with Two Year olds*; Department of Education, Northern Ireland; 2008

Euridice; 'Compulsory age of starting school in European countries', NFER Nelson; 2010

Garhart Mooney, Carol; *Theories of Childhood*; Redleaf Press; 2000

Goldschmeid, Elinor and Jackson, Sonia; *People Under Three*; Routledge; 1994

Gopnik, Alison et al; *How Babies Think*; Phoenix; 2001

Gopnik, Alison; *The Philosophical Baby*; Bodley Head; 2009

Greenman, Jim; *Caring Spaces, Learning Places*; Exchange Press; 2005

Greenman, Jim and Stonehouse, Anne; *Prime Times*; Redleaf Press; 1996

Hall, John; Spotlight 92, Neuroscience and education; 'What can brain science contribute to teaching and learning?' University of Gasgow; 2005

Hays, Sharon. *The Cultural Contradictions of Motherhood*; New Haven, CT: Yale University Press, 1996

Healey, Jane; *Your Child's Growing Mind*; Broadway; 2004

Hohmann, Mary and Weikart, David P; *Educating Young Children*; High/Scope Press; 2002

Institute of Education, University of London and Department for Education and Skills; Effective Provision of Pre-School Education (EPPE) Technical Paper 12 – 'The final report: Effective Pre-school Education'; 2004

Kinsley, Craig H. PhD, and Meyer, Elizabeth A. PhD, 'The Plasticity of the Human Maternal Brain: Longitudinal Changes in Brain Anatomy During the Early Postpartum Period': Theoretical Comment on Kim et al. (2010), University of Richmond; *Behavioral Neuroscience*, Vol. 124, No. 5, (quoted in *Scientific American Mind*, April 2011)

Learning and Teaching Scotland; *Curriculum for Excellence Through Outdoor Learning*; 2010)

Learning and Teaching Scotland; *Pre-Birth to Three; Positive outcomes for Scotland's Children and their Families*; 2010

Lindon, Jennie; 'Good practice in working with babies, toddlers and very young children'; *www.peelearlyyears.com*

Lindon, Jennie; Kelman, Kevin; Sharp, Alice; 'Play and Learning for the Under Threes'; *Nursery World*; 2001

Louv Richard; *The Last Child in the Woods*; Algonquin Paperbacks; 2005

Ministry of Social Affairs and Health; 'Early Childhood Education and Care in Finland'; Brochures of the Ministry of Social Affairs and Health; 2004: No.14

Montessori, Maria; *Dr Montessori's own Handbook*; Schocken Books, 1965

National Scientific Council on the Developing Child; *The Science of Early Childhood Development: Closing the gap between what we know and what we do*; Harvard University; 2007; http://www.developingchild.net

National School Improvement Network 'Research Matters' No 21, The Effective Provision of Pre-school Education (EPPE) Project; Institute of Education; University of London; 2003

New Zealand Government; *Te Whariki Early Childhood Curriculum*; Ministry of Education; Learning Media; Wellington; 1996

Office for Standards in Education; *Evaluation Schedule for Schools*; (OFSTED, UK); January 2011.

OWP/P Architects; *The Third Teacher: 79 Ways You Can Use Design to Transform Teaching and Learning*; Abrams; 2010

Play Wales; *Richer Play in Schools*; 2005

Post, Jacalyn and Hohmann, Mary; *Tender Care and Early Learning*; High/Scope Press; 2000

Purvis, Andrew; 'Battery versus Barn'; The Guardian on Line 2006

Roberts, Rosemary; *Wellbeing from Birth*; Sage; 2010

Rodd, Jillian; *Understanding Young Children's Behaviour*; Teachers College Press; 1996

Rousseau, Jean Jacques; *Emile*; (1762); Everyman Library; 2000

Royal Society for the Protection of Birds/English Nature; *Every Child Outdoors*; 2010

Forest Research/Forestry Commission; Offenders and Nature; www.forestresearch.gov.uk/offendersandnature

Rumbold, Angela; *Starting with Quality*; Department for Education; 1990

Sinclair, Alan; *0-5: How Small Children Make a Big Difference*; The Work Foundation; 2007 Sylva et al; *Assessing Quality in the Early Years: Early Childhood Environment Rating Scale* (ECERS-E); Trentham Books; 2003

Sylva et al; *Effective Provision of Pre-School Education* (EPPE), Institute of Education; London; 1999/2003/2004

Tickell, Dame Clare; *The Early Years: Foundations for life, health and learning*; An Independent Report on the Early Years Foundation Stage to Her Majesty's Government; March 2011

National Scientific Council on the Developing Child; 'The Timing and Quality of Early Years Experiences Combine to Shape Brain Architecture'; Working Paper 5; Harvard University; 2008

UNICEF, *The Child Care Transition*, Innocenti Report Card 8,; Innocenti Research Centre, Florence, 2008

Valentine, Marianne; *The Reggio Approach to Early Years Education*; Scottish Consultative Council on the Curriculum; 1999

Walsh, G. et al; *Thinking Skills for the Early Years: A Guide for Practitioners*; Stranmills University College; Belfast; 2005

Welsh Assembly Government; *Observing Children*; 2008

International Froebel Society; www.intfroebelsoc.org

http://www.scribd.com/doc/13401568/Piaget-Versus-Vygotsky

http://www.dailymail.co.uk/news/article-462091/How-children-lost-right-roam-generations.html